10 20

THE
1914
CAMPAIGN

French Schneider P.B.2 buses, taken off the streets of Paris to bring supplies to Compiègne. The buses' distinctive rear platforms are clearly visible here.

The Great Military Campaigns of History★

THE 1914 CAMPAIGN

August - October, 1914

Daniel David

Military Press
New York

This book is dedicated to Field Marshal Sir Henry H. Wilson,
Chief-of-the-Imperial General Staff, 1918–1922

Acknowledgments

A number of people helped make this book possible. Joseph Ward was of great assistance in assembling materials for the project.

I particularly want to thank both Robert Pigeon of Combined Books and Albert Nofi, the general editor of The Great Campaigns of Military History, for their patience, kindness, and confidence in me.

DANIEL DAVID
New York
10 April 1987

The illustrations in this book have been reproduced from a private collection supplied by the author. The original photos were all taken in 1914, primarily by photographers for British news organizations. The following illustrations were obtained by kind permission of other agencies: J.H. Beers Collection, page 97 (top left and bottom), page 98 (top right); Military Archives and Research Services, page 98-99 (background, courtesy of the Imperial War Museum), front and back jacket photos. Other color photographs were supplied through private collections. Credit for other illustrations appear in the text. The maps were obtained with the permission of Hippocrene Books, Inc.

Prepared by Combined Books
26 Summit Grove, Suite 207
Bryn Mawr, PA 19010

Project Director: Robert L. Pigeon
Project Coordinator: Antoinette Bauer
Editor of the Series: Albert A. Nofi
Photographic Research: Kenneth S. Gallagher
Layout: Tracy Reeser, Lizbeth Hoefer-Nauta

Produced by Wieser and Wieser, Inc.
118 East 25th Street, New York, NY 10010.

This 1987 edition published by Military Press
Distributed by Crown Publishers, Inc.
225 Park Avenue South
New York, New York 10003

h g f e d c b a

ISBN 0-517-64158-5

ege Fort Loncin after German bombardment.

Contents

PREFACE TO THE SERIES

Jonathan Swift termed war "that mad game the world so loves to play". He had a point. Universally condemned, it has nevertheless been almost as universally practiced. For good or ill, war has played a significant role in the shaping of history. Indeed, there is hardly a human institution which has not in some fashion been influenced and molded by war, even as it helped shape and mold war in turn. Yet the study of war has been as remarkably neglected as its practice has been commonplace. With a few outstanding exceptions, the history of wars and of military operations has until quite recently been largely the province of the inspired patriot or the regimental polemicist. Only in our times have serious, detailed, and objective accounts come to be considered the norm in the treatment of military history and related matters. Yet there still remains a gap in the literature, for there are two types of military history. One type is written from a very serious, highly technical, professional perspective and presupposes that the reader is deeply familiar with background, technology, and general situation. The other is perhaps less dry, but merely lightly reviews the events with the intention of informing and entertaining the layman. The qualitative gap between the two is vast. Moreover, there are professionals in both the military and in academia whose credentials are limited to particular moments in the long, sad history of war, and there are laymen who have a more than passing understanding of the field; and then there is the concerned citizen, interested in understanding the phenomenon in an age of unusual violence and unprecedented armaments. It is to bridge the gap between the two types of military history, and to reach the professional and the serious amateur and the concerned citizen alike, that this series, *The Great Campaigns of Military History*, is designed.

The individual volumes of *The Great Campaigns of Military History* are each devoted to an intensive examination of a particularly significant military operation. The focus is not on individual battles, but on campaigns, on the relationship between movements and battles and how they fit within the overall framework of the war in question. By making use of a series of innovative techniques for the presentation of information, *The Great Campaigns of Military History* can satisfy the exacting demands of the professional and the serious amateur, while making it possible for the concerned citizen to understand the events and the conditions under which they developed. This is accomplished in a number of ways. Each volume contains a substantial, straight-forward narrative account of the campaign under study. This is supported by an extensive series of modular "sidebars". Some are devoted to particular specific technical matters, such as weaponry, logistics, organization, or tactics. These modules each contain detailed analyses of their topic, and make considerable use of "hard" data, with many charts and tables. Other modules deal with less technical matters, such as strategic analysis, anecdotes, personalities, uniforms, and politics. Each volume contains several detailed maps, supplemented by a number of clear, accurate sketchmaps, which assist the reader in understanding the course of events under consideration, and there is an extensive set of illustrations which have been selected to assist the reader still further. Finally, each volume contains materials designed to help the reader who is interested in learning more. But this "bibliography" includes not merely a short list of books and articles related to the campaign in question. It also contains information on study groups devoted to the subject, on films which deal with it, on recordings of period music, on simulation games and skirmish clubs which attempt to recreate the tactics, on museums where one can have a first-hand look at equipment, and on tours of the battlefields. The particular contents of each volume will, of course, be determined by the topic in question, but each will provide an unusually rich and varied treatment of the subject. Each volume in *The Great Campaigns of Military History* is thus not merely an account of a particular military operation, but it is a unique reference to the theory and practice of war in the period in question.

The Great Campaigns of Military History is a unique contribution to the study of war and of military history, which will remain of interest and use for many years.

German 77mm guns captured by the British at the Marne.

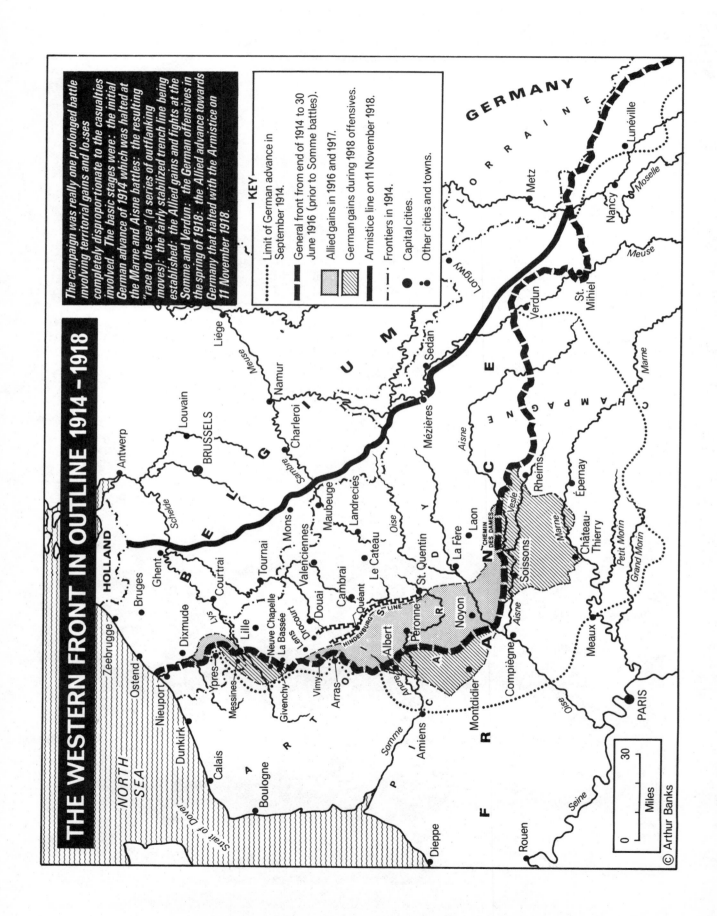

THE WESTERN FRONT IN OUTLINE 1914–1918

The campaign was really one prolonged battle involving territorial gains and losses completely disproportionate to the casualties involved. The basic stages were: the initial German advance of 1914 which was halted at the Marne and Aisne battles: the resulting "race to the sea" (a series of outflanking moves): the fairly stabilized trench line being established: the Allied gains and fights at the Somme and Verdun: the German offensives in the spring of 1918: the Allied advance towards Germany that halted with the Armistice on 11 November 1918.

KEY

Limit of German advance in September 1914.

General front from end of 1914 to 30 June 1916 (prior to Somme battles).

Allied gains in 1916 and 1917.

German gains during 1918 offensives.

Armistice line on 11 November 1918.

Frontiers in 1914.

Capital cities.

Other cities and towns.

GERMANY

LORRAINE

Lunéville

Moselle

Metz

Nancy

Meuse

Longwy

Verdun

St. Mihiel

Liége

Meuse

Namur

Sedan

Mézières

Charleroi

Aisne

Louvain

BRUSSELS

B E L G I U M

Sambre

Antwerp

HOLLAND

Schelde

Ghent

Bruges

Zeebrugge

Ostend

Nieuport

Dunkirk

Calais

Boulogne

NORTH SEA

Strait of Dover

Dieppe

Rouen

Seine

F R A N C E

Amiens

Somme

Montdidier

Compiègne

Oise

PARIS

Meaux

Grand Morin

Petit Morin

Château-Thierry

Marne

Épernay

Rheims

Vesle

Soissons

CHEMIN DES DAMES

Aisne

Laon

La Fère

Noyon

St. Quentin

Péronne

Albert

Ancre

HINDENBURG LINE

Quéant

Cambrai

Le Cateau

Oise

Douai

Arras

Vimy

Lens

Givenchy

Drocourt

La Bassée

Neuve Chapelle

Lille

Messines

Ypres

Dixmude

Lys

Courtrai

Tournai

Valenciennes

Mons

Maubeuge

Landrecies

C H A M P A G N E

30

Miles

0

© Arthur Banks

Introduction

The Campaign of 1914 turned the world upside down. Every nation involved was drastically changed. Touched off by the assassination of the Austrian heir, Archduke Franz Ferdinand, by Gavrilo Princip, a Serbian nationalist, at Sarajevo on June 28, the campaign signaled the end of an era. The great dynasties of Eastern and Central Europe, the heyday of the aristocrats—those great families with names like Romanov, Habsburg, and Hohenzollern—were all swept away. It marked the end of European predominance in the world political arena and the beginning of global politics. It paved the way for the dissolution of colonial empires, led communism to triumph in Russia, and America to enter the global arena. The political tensions of the world today are in many ways a direct result of the campaign of 1914.

From a military perspective the campaign of 1914 is significant because never before had strategies been so minutely and elaborately planned. It seemed to those in charge that every contingency had been accounted for and every man knew what he was supposed to do when mobilization occurred. Thus, every German man of military age had a card in his possession telling him the exact steps to follow once Germany declared war. The Germans planned to defeat France in the remarkable period of six weeks during the warm, dry summer months of August and September. Nevertheless, despite the most elaborate strategies ever devised, the meticulously planned campaign ended in the trenches. Long years of stalemate followed, with cold, wet, sick soldiers suffering for months in trenches and advances which could be measured in feet. None of this had been part

of anyone's plans: the brilliant colors of the uniforms were not supposed to be encrusted with mud. Yet in many ways this outcome was inherent in the plans.

The Campaign of 1914 ushered in the era of total war. Whole societies mobilized to pursue victory. It introduced new weapons and tactics, offensive as well as defensive, aerial reconnaissance and observation of troop movements, propaganda, barbed wire, motorization, trenches, machine-guns—all were dominant factors—along with mud.

By 1914 war had been anticipated and feared and sought after for over a generation. Both France and Germany had evolved highly complex strategies for invading each other. The Germans were prepared to use the Schlieffen Plan, the creation of Chief-of-the-General Staff Alfred von Schlieffen. Despite France's Russian Alliance and the consequent threat from the East, the Germans had decided that France was still the primary enemy. They also knew that the French must be beaten and put out of the war before the Russians could mass their huge armies. The original plan called for a simultaneous invasion of the Netherlands, Belgium, and Luxembourg, by the bulk of the German armies, thus taking the French armies in their left flank. An admitted violation of neutral territories, the move was believed essential to national survival. The successor to Schlieffen as Chief-of-the-General Staff, Helmuth von Moltke the Younger, changed the original plan somewhat in the light of changing political realities. He decided that only Belgium and Luxembourg need be invaded and he also strengthened the number of corps on the opposite flank.

SCHLIEFFEN, MOLTKE, AND GERMAN MILITARY PLANNING: A CRITIQUE.

Modern Germany was created in 1871, when the Second German Reich was proclaimed at Versailles. Prussia had fought three short wars to accomplish this feat, The Danish War of 1864, The Austrian War of 1866 and The Franco-Prussian War of 1870–71. A new and powerful state now joined the order of European states. The architects of this new entity were Count Otto von Bismarck, the Chancellor (1815–1898), General Albert von Roon (1803–1879), the War Minister, and General Helmuth von Moltke (1801–1891), the Chief-of-the-General Staff.

The foreign policy and the military policy of Bismarckian Germany were similar, to try for a reconciliation with France, while encouraging France's quest for colonial empire, and pursuing peaceful relations with a fellow conservative state, Russia. Moltke stated quite frankly that the new German state should avoid any two front wars at all costs. Germany was militarily a powerful state, but manpower and resources were not infinite, and neither was the public purse. But by the early 1890s everything began to come apart. France proved intransigent, the Russians found a new ally in France, and even Britain became unfriendly.

What had gone wrong? It was the new Kaiser Wilhelm II (reigned

1880–1918). The unstable, young, and ambitious Wilhelm fired the ancient and wise Bismarck, while age and mortality took away Moltke in 1891. Wilhelm took control. The new German Empire

Count Otto von Bismark, architect of the Second Reich. His refusal to incorporate Austria in the German Empire left a dangerous neighbor on its eastern border.

was much like a ship with a faulty steering in a body of water with strong but conflicting currents. Bismarck's foreign policy was thrown over with disastrous results. France became increasingly antago-

nistic, while the Germans alienated Russia by cultivating Austria-Hungary as an ally. The result was the Franco-Russian Alliance of 1892. Germany meanwhile antagonized Great Britain by its behavior in encouraging anti-British feelings throughout Europe during the Anglo-Boer War (1899–1902). The crowning blunder was the Kaiser's desire for a great navy, a goal which could only be viewed with trepidation in Britain.

In 1891 General Count Alfred von Schlieffen (1833–1913) took up the position as chief-of-the-general staff. A firm believer in the value of studying and teaching military history, Schlieffen held that past experiences could help the staff officer in his present duties. He had become captivated, and eventually obsessed, with the battle of Cannae, the battle in which Hannibal annihilated the Roman Army and its allied forces. In 1909, four years after his retirement, he wrote in a letter, "The battle of annihilation alone is the desirable battle." Schlieffen wished to eliminate Germany's most powerful enemy, France, in a single crushing campaign. It must be quick: 1870–71 took one year, with Russia now in the picture Germany did not have the time.

Schlieffen was a great theorist and embarked upon his plans with tremendous energy and intelligence.

von Falkenhayn as Minister of War.

Schlieffen was anxious to deploy his armies in a manner which would gain an advantage of maneuver on a wide scale. Germany would have to violate the neutrality of both Holland and Belgium. He even considered a possible movement through Switzerland, but the defensive strength of the country counted against this. The province of Limberg in Holland would be crossed by German troops and all of Belgium would be invaded. He made no account of the fact that the German state of Prussia had been a guarantor of Belgian neutrality in 1839, and that the new German State had assumed that obligation. In effect, by invading Belgium in 1914 the Germans handed the Asquith Government an easy entry to aid France in the war.

Schlieffen planned to move a strong force through Limberg in Holland and Northern Belgium.

Thus, the Right Wing of the German Army, was divided into three parts. On the extreme right he deployed five cavalry divisions, seventeen army corps (including reserve corps, in a daring but brilliant move), and six ersatz corps which were assembled and deployed upon mobilization, plus a number of *Landwehr* and *Landstrum* brigades. These forces were to deploy in the sector opposite Brussels-Namur, cross the Somme between Abbeville and Chaules, pass westward of Paris, and then move in an easterly direction into the flank and rear of the French Armies.

The central group of the right wing was to deploy in the area Namur-Mezieres, with a cavalry division, six army corps, and several Landwehr brigades, to advance in close contact with the far right wing between, Chaules

Berliners cheer at the announcement of war.

However, he lived the life of a Prussian officer, keeping away from the world of politics and of industry. This great plan, which, though compiled by hand, can rival any modern computer generated strategy, with its intricate mobilization tables and railway movements, would lead to disaster.

Even in the world of theory Schlieffen had problems. The Cannae concept overlooked the political world of the Roman Republic. While their field army was virtually destroyed, the government and the population were determined to form new armies and fight on. They did and they won the war. The idea of winning a war by a single brilliant stroke is intoxicating, as a mirage is to a desert traveler. In modern warfare we are faced with annihilation but not victory.

Belgian refugees. An all-too-familiar sight for the rest of the century.

and La Fere, and attack the French Army where Schlieffen thought they would be, on the Oise between La Fere and Paris. The left flank of the right wing would comprise two cavalry divisions, eight active corps and five reserve corps (including the garrison and main reserve of Metz), and some Landwehr brigades. This army would be located opposite Mezieres-Verdun, and was expected to engage the French Army on the Aisne and Aire, on the line La Fere-Verdun, to move south enveloping Verdun from the west of the Meuse.

The left wing of the German armies, the fourth group of Schlieffen's plan, was to comprise three cavalry divisions, three active corps and three reserve corps plus two ersatz corps. They were to deploy east of the Moselle opposite Verdun-Nancy in order to tie down as much of the French Forces as possible. South of Strabourg there would be, of German troops, only three and one half Landwehr

brigades covering the upper Rhine, but bolstered by as many as five Italian army corps.

Basically the German right wing would wheel westwards, southwards, and then eastwards, around the pivot of Metz-Thionville and sweep the French Army against Switzerland.

In 1912 Schlieffen made suggestions to improve upon the plan:

1) Extend the right wing to swing out far beyond Paris, up to the coast of France.

2) Engage the enemy along the whole front to pin his forces and to uncover weak points.

3) Reorganize the army, abandon the corps concept and replace it with a new type of division.

On 1 January 1905 General Helmuth von Moltke, a nephew of the Great Moltke, succeeded Colonel-General Alfred von Schlieffen as Chief-of-the-General Staff. The Younger Moltke has been generally

villified in the German military literature of the post-war years. Many of the leading critics were followers of Schlieffen and had served on his staff.

As chief-of-the-general staff, the Younger Moltke was fully justified in making any changes that he wanted in Schlieffen's plan. In 1909, aware than an Italian presence on his left was increasingly unlikely, he decided to change the ratio of the German troops between the right wing and the left wing. He rearranged the forces on the left wing by creating the *Sixth* and the *Seventh Armies* in Alsace and Lorraine. Moltke's action was based on intelligence reports that the French Army was no longer going to restrict itself to a defensive strategy, but would go over to the offensive probably against Alsace-Lorraine and the Upper Rhine. Moltke had to consider the defense of Southern Germany and the

von Moltke. His fellow officers criticized him for altering the Schlieffen Plan.

Krupp works at Essen.

industrial areas on the Rhine. Neither Erich Ludendorff, who was then head of the Operations Department, nor Wilhelm Groener, Chief of the Railway Department, objected to these changes.

Moltke has been accused of weakening the right wing. This is unfair. Schlieffen's formations were frequently paper ones, his assumptions often visionary. Moltke had to deal with political and diplomatic realities and with genuine units. He actually increased the strength of the German forces, particularly on the right. Two more active corps were created, a number of reserve divisions were enlarged and new

Skilled German bridging troops were essential for a rapid advance through Belgium and France.

Russian Minister of War Sukhomlinoff

von Hindenburg, commanding the German armies on the Eastern Front.

reserve corps were created. Moltke still approved of the invasion of Belgium. However, Holland would remain neutral, to conserve manpower. Schlieffen had believed that the French would stay behind their line of fortifications in Eastern France. Moltke thought otherwise and was right; the French did launch an offensive. In addition, the Germans were under considerable pressure from the Austrians to send additional troops to the East as soon as possible. In 1914 Moltke was also pressured by Hindenberg and Ludendorff for additional troops. On 26 August he gave in, and on the fall of Namur he ordered the *Guards Reserve Corps* and the *IX Corps* to be transferred East. He had hoped to transfer a total of six corps to the east. The Germans had one corps laying siege to Maubeuge and later two corps doing the same to Antwerp. As August turned to September the strength of the German Army started to diminish. As Napoleon had once remarked, "A General should consider himself successful if half of what he plans comes to pass." The Schlieffen Plan assumed everything would go perfectly, a formula for disaster.

"A SHILLING A DAY, BLOOMIN' GOOD PAY—" MONTHLY RECRUIT SALARIES, 1914

Since the Continental armies relied upon conscription, they were able to pay their troops very little by comparison with the all-volunteer American and British forces. Switzerland, which was the only genuine nation in arms at time, paid its sturdy militiamen even less, $0.16 a month. In order to make comparisons easier these figures have been converted into American money of 1914, at a time when a laborer's wage in the U.S. was about $0.10 an hour. For a very rough idea of the purchasing power of these sums in terms of the late 1980s, multiply by 36.

ARMY	PAY
Austro-Hungarian	$ .73
British	8.56
French	1.70
German	3.21
Russian	.32
U.S.	15.00

The Austrians' beloved Emperor Franz Josef. His reign from 1848 to 1916 was one of Europe's longest.

The Grand Duchess Marie Adelaide of Luxemburg. The Germans occupied Luxemburg on August 1, 1914.

The French army had plans of their own. After the turn of the century they decided to drop their former defensive strategy and concentrate on the attack. Their old strategy had called for them to concentrate their armies around frontier fortresses and await the Germans. Their new strategy, called Plan 17, was an offensive strategy. A major objective of the new Plan 17 was to retake the provinces lost to Germany in the humiliation of 1871, Alsace and Lorraine. But the French knew what the Germans were up to and planned to stop a German attack by attacking. They had obtained a copy of the German plan in 1904. As a result, they made some changes in the disposition of the frontier forces: the Fifth Army was moved closer to the border with Luxembourg and Belgium. The French planned to attack the German armies on their flank as they moved into Belgium.

Both armies entered the war with a plan. The strains and uncertainties of wartime operations, in the clash with reality, proved both plans unworkable. They would destroy the reputations of the military leaders who strove to implement them. In Germany the Chief-of-the-General Staff was the real commander. Helmuth von Moltke, sixty-six years old when the war started, was a sensitive, intelligent man without real iron in his character. The Imperial German Army and its leaders had not seen combat in a major war since 1870-1871, when Helmuth von Moltke the Elder had led them to glory over France. They had some limited participation in the suppression of the Boxer Rebellion and the crushing of a local revolt in South West Africa, but experience of this sort did not apply to conditions in Europe. The French Army had recent experience in colonial warfare. Its commander, General Joseph Joffre, was a prominent colonial soldier. But he was answerable to several higher authorities less in touch with contemporary warfare technique, and he himself lacked imagination, though commendably tough. The commander of the British Expeditionary Force was Field Marshal Sir John French, who despite his name, spoke little French. The manner in which he handled his troops in the field demonstrated that he was not up to the requirements of modern warfare and active service. Thus, all three armies were led by men of little genius, a fact which would bulk large in the course of events. Not one of the supreme commanders of the Campaign of 1914 lasted more than two years. Their failure in command set the pattern for what was to come, not merely in the war itself, but for the balance of the century.

The super-battleship H.M.S. Dreadnought. *Anglo-German naval rivalry was a direct cause of the war.*

Kaiser Wilhelm II, King George's first cousin.

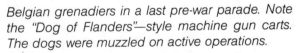

Belgian grenadiers in a last pre-war parade. Note the "Dog of Flanders"—style machine gun carts. The dogs were muzzled on active operations.

French infantry on the way to the front. France's "vitalist" philosophers had convinced the General Staff that red trousers were essential for victory.

The younger von Moltke. A man with a deep spiritual sense, this nephew of Bismarck's general was mentally unprepared for the carnage of modern warfare.

Field Marshall Sir John French. His relief expeditions in the Boer War had taught him the value, and difficulties, of rapid maneuver.

Joffre

LOGISTICS OF THE CAMPAIGN OF 1914

Historically the organization of the movements and supply of an army has always been among the most difficult, if least obvious, of the commander's tasks. By 1914 these had become even more difficult and complex, due partially to the effects of the increasing technologization of warfare and partially to the remarkably intricate mobilization plans favored by all of the powers. What follows is a series of examples designed to suggest the complexity of the problems involved in the new war.

Mobilization

To move a single combat-ready German regular army corps from its depot to its deployment area necessitated 280 trains. These comprised over 12000 wagons, of which

170 were passenger carriages for officers,

965 were freight wagons for troops,

2960 were specially fitted wagons for horses,

1915 were flat cars or freight wagons for artillery and impedimenta, and

c. 6000 were freight wagons for ammunition, food, fodder, and supplies.

Now, consider that the German Army mobilized 42 active and reserve army corps in only 15 days at the onset of the war. There was thus a total requirement for some 11,000 trains comprising over 460,000 railroad wagons. Nor do these figures take into account the mobilization of *landwehr*, replacement, and naval personnel.

Rations

Most of the 1914 armies managed to provide their troops with a nutritious and rather varied diet, certainly in comparison to that which earlier generations of soldiers had been content with. The French ration may be taken as fairly typical.

Each day, each man in the French Army was supposed to receive:

750 gr of bread or 700 of biscuit ("hard tack")

500 gr of fresh or tinned meat ("bully beef")

30 gr of lard or 50 gr of salt pork

100 gr of potato or carrots or legumes

20 gr of salt

24 gr of coffee

32 gr of sugar

.25 liter of *Pinaud* [*vin très ordinaire*]

In addition, there was a weekly issue of 100 grams of tobacco. The rations of the other armies were pretty much similar to the French, though with variations suited to their national culinary proclivities. Thus, the Germans gave their men only 410 grammes of bread and biscuit, but fully 500 grammes of potatoes, while the Belgians surprisingly had an issue of milk rather than alcohol. Feeding the troops required an enormous investment in manpower and equipment. The standard French field bakery, with 40 bakers and 22 other personnel, could produce 2,000 bread rations every 24 hours working at maximum effort. More realistically, there was one such bakery for each battalion, so that

there were over 30 in each army corps, requiring a total of nearly 2000 men, about 4% of T/O&E strength.

The experience of the war caused most powers to alter the composition of their standard fare in some details, but the 1918 rations were essentially similar to those of 1914, save in one area, alcoholic beverages. The French would double their daily ration of wine by the war's end, having discovered that it helped a lot.

Now, the weight of all this food works out to a daily total of between 1.69 and 1.72 kilograms per man. With packaging included, this means that between 95 and 101 tonnes of food were required each day for each army corps. But feeding the men was by no means as difficult a task as feeding the horses.

The standard horse ration of 1914 was about 10 kilograms of feed and fodder each day. The German *First Army*, which required about 555 tons of food each day for its 260,000 men also needed some 840 tons of feed and fodder for its 84,000 horses. To put it another way, the *First Army* needed 50% more food for horses than for men, though it had over three times as many men as horses. Supplying food for horses even exceeded the requirements of supplying food for guns. In the course of the war, the British were to ship to France 25,500,000 tons of supplies and equipment. Only 5,250,000 tons (20.6%) of this was in the form of ammunition, while over 6,000,000 tons (23.5%) were feed and fodder for horses and mules.

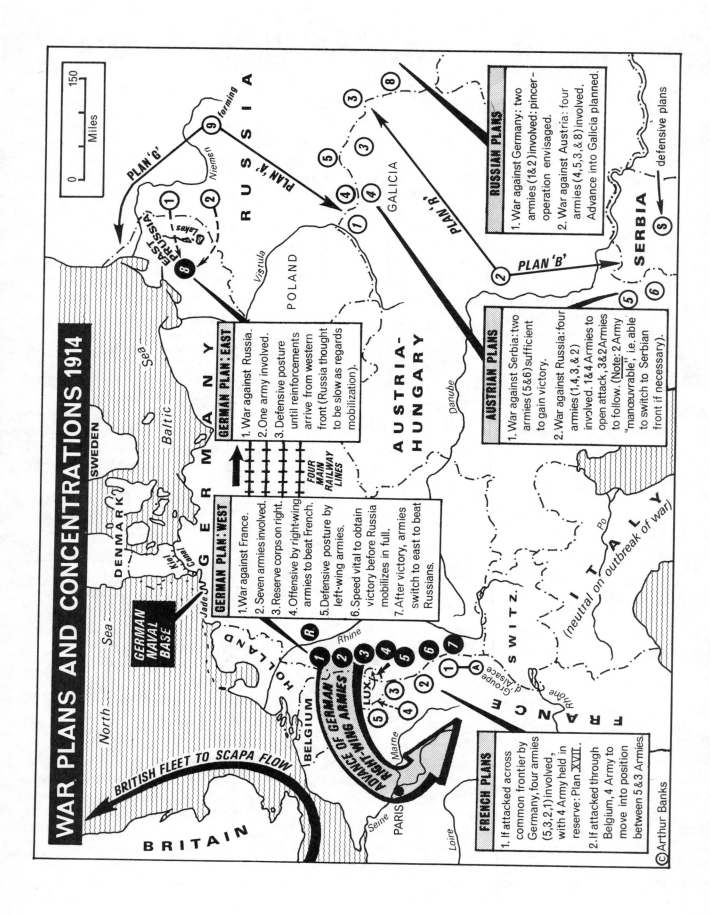

WAR PLANS AND CONCENTRATIONS 1914

GERMAN NAVAL BASE

BRITISH FLEET TO SCAPA FLOW

PLAN 'G'

PLAN 'A'

PLAN 'R'

PLAN 'B'

FOUR MAIN RAILWAY LINES

ADVANCE OF GERMAN ARMIES

RIGHT-WING

GERMAN PLAN: EAST
1. War against Russia.
2. One army involved.
3. Defensive posture until reinforcements arrive from western front (Russia thought to be slow as regards mobilization).

GERMAN PLAN: WEST
1. War against France.
2. Seven armies involved.
3. Reserve corps on right.
4. Offensive by right-wing armies to beat French.
5. Defensive posture by left-wing armies.
6. Speed vital to obtain victory before Russia mobilizes in full.
7. After victory, armies switch to east to beat Russians.

RUSSIAN PLANS
1. War against Germany: two armies (1&2) involved: pincer-operation envisaged.
2. War against Austria: four armies (4,5,3,&8) involved. Advance into Galicia planned.

AUSTRIAN PLANS
1. War against Serbia: two armies (5&6) sufficient to gain victory.
2. War against Russia: four armies (1,4,3,& 2) involved. 1&4 Armies to open attack, 3&2 Armies to follow. (Note: 2 Army "manoeuvrable", i.e. able to switch to Serbian front if necessary).

FRENCH PLANS
1. If attacked across common frontier by Germany, four armies (5,3,2,1) involved, with 4 Army held in reserve: Plan XVII.
2. If attacked through Belgium, 4 Army to move into position between 5 &3 Armies.

SWEDEN

DENMARK

Kiel Canal
Jade

North Sea

Baltic Sea

HOLLAND

BELGIUM

LUX.

GERMANY

POLAND

RUSSIA

EAST PRUSSIA

Lakes

Niemen

Vistula

GALICIA

AUSTRIA-HUNGARY

Danube

SWITZ.

ITALY

Po

(neutral on outbreak of war)

FRANCE

BRITAIN

PARIS

Seine

Marne

Loire

Rhine

Rhône

Groupe d'Alsace

SERBIA

defensive plans

R

© Arthur Banks

CHAPTER I

THE OPENING MOVES

IT began with an assassination, not an unusual event even in the 'Gilded Age.' Europe received the news of Sarajevo with remarkable calm. No one seemed concerned and life went on as before. But in Vienna, ineptitude and arrogance combined towards the end of July to spark a crisis with Serbia. Nations began to grow worried. In late July the Belgian government, unofficially aware of the details of the Schlieffen Plan, became increasingly concerned with the deterioration of the political situation in Europe. At 2300 on 29 July 1914, the day after Austria-Hungary declared war on Serbia, the Minister of War gave orders that all garrisons were to be placed on reinforcement status by calling up reserve forces. On 31 July Germany declared a Precautionary Alert and closed the frontier between the two countries. The situation became very grave. At 2400 on 1 August the Belgian government ordered a general mobilization. King Albert, a tall, handsome, awkward-looking young man who would prove to have enormous courage and will power, asked the original guarantors of the 1839 Treaty of London, which neutralized Belgium "in perpetuity," for reassurances concerning Belgium status. It was especially important to secure this from the three signers of the treaty who were contiguous to Belgium's frontiers, France, Britain, and Germany. Belgium was open to acts of hostility by any of these nations and some sort of affirmation would be of value. It was perhaps a thin reed to lean on, however, so with the German closing of the frontier, the Belgians put their Plan 1 into effect. Plan 1 involved preparations for a possible violation of Belgian territory by Germany. Under Plan 1, the Field Army was to be concentrated east of the Gette River. Meanwhile, aided by his German-born wife, King Albert addressed a final, personal appeal for peace to the Kaiser. Wilhelm II ignored him. The German 'response' came at 1900 on 2 August, in the form of an ultimatum delivered to the Foreign Office by the German Ambassador.

Germany demanded that her armies have free passage through Belgium and the unlimited use of the Belgian railway network. It was a deadly offer. If the Belgians agreed to such an arrangement they would be violating their status as a neutral, committing an act hostile to France. This would leave them open to French military action and to a hostile British reaction as well. Moreover, if Belgium agreed the country would be overrun by German armies. The ultimatum was rejected.

At 0802 on 4 August 1914 the vanguard of the German Army moved into Belgium. This was a force of six infantry brigades and the *II Cavalry Corps* under Gen. Otto von Emmich. Emmich's mission was to invest the fortress of Liege and secure the flanks of the German *First* and *Second Armies* as they moved to implement the initial phase of the Schlieffen Plan, setting the stage for the turning movement through Belgium. The German troops moved to surround the ring of 12 forts which protected Liege. Liege was a bottle neck through which the Germans intended to funnel 520,000 men. It was protected by a defensive system designed by the famous engineer Alexis Brialmont between 1888 and 1892. The forts, carefully sited to cover the approaches to the city, were mutually supporting, each having eight pieces of artillery in cupolas. However, only two of three of these guns were long range 210mm pieces, the rest were 120 or 150mm guns. The forts were supported by 75mm guns and infantry posted in outer works. Altogether, the garrison numbered some 40,000 men, including the 3rd Division under Gen. Gerard Leman, a distinguished member of the Belgian War College and King Albert's military mentor. The forts were secure against the standard 77mm field gun of the German Army, even against 150mm field guns. However, they were constructed of unreinforced concrete and had not been modernized, and thus were not proof against the new very heavy artillery.

Albert, King of the Belgians. This official portrait omits the scholarly glasses he often wore.

The Franco-Belgian railroad net was a prime target of the German advance.

Liege

Belgian cavalry scouts on the Waterloo battlefield. Their green coats and red trousers would have made them more visible than the Germans they were seeking.

AVAILABILITY OF INFANTRY DIVISIONS THE WESTERN FRONT 1914

Week		The Allies				The Germans			Ger Army as a % of Allies
	Belg	Brit	Fr	Tot		Tot	West	%	
Aug 2	6		75	81		83	71	85.5	87.7%
9	6		79	85		83	71	85.5	83.5
16	6	4	79	89		83	71	85.5	79.8
23	6	4	85	95		83	71	85.5	74.7
30	6	5	85	96		83	69	83.1	71.9
Sep 6	6	5	85	96		89	73	82.0	76.0
13	6	6	86	98		89	73	82.0	74.5
20	6	6	87	99		89	73	82.0	73.7
27	6	7	89	102		89	74	82.2	72.5
Oct 4	6	7	88	101		89	74	82.2	73.3
11	6	9	88	103		91	75	82.4	71.4
18	6	10	88	104		103	85	82.5	81.7
25	6	10	88	104		103	85	82.5	82.5
Nov 1	6	10	90	106		104	86	82.7	81.1
8	6	10	89	105		104	86	82.7	81.9
15	6	10	88	104		105	87	82.9	83.7
22	6	10	88	104		105	87	82.9	83.7
29	6	10	88	104		105	87	82.9	83.7
Dec 6	6	10	88	104		112	91	81.3	86.5
13	6	10	89	105		112	91	81.3	85.7
20	6	10	89	105		112	87	77.6	81.9
27	6	11	89	106		112	87	77.6	81.1

In 1914 the contemporary way of calculating military power was in terms of divisions, and specifically of infantry divisions. This table presents a summary of the divisions available to each of the Western Front combatants at the start of each week from the onset of mobilization to the end of December. All types of infantry divisions have been included here, those of the active armies, plus reserve, territorial, and *Landwehr* formations, with two exceptions: the three Belgian fortress divisions (Antwerp, Liege, and Namur), and the six German *Ersatzheer* "corps," which were supposed to be mobile replacement formations; they did, in fact, eventually enter the line. No attempt has been made to estimate the divisional equivalents tied up to independent brigades, none of which had any support services or artillery: Germany had 27 such brigades, all of *Landwehr* or *Landsturm*, while France had five and Britain one, all of regulars. Forces not present in the theater of operations are omitted. For the British this means all forces in the United Kingdom, for France divisions on the Italian frontier, until these were withdrawn beginning in Mid-April, and those in North Africa. German figures include the total number of infantry divisions available, the number committed to the Western Front, and the percentage which this constituted of the total.

Changes in the numbers of divisions are due to a variety of factors. An increase indicates the arrival of new divisions from overseas or the activation of new formations, while a decrease may be due to the movement of formations overseas—the French had to replace active army formations in North Africa with territorials—or to the administrative dissolution of a division. Note that these are net figures, thus, although the French raised two new divisions in the week ending 6 September, they also disbanded two, with the result that no change in the number of divisions is shown for that week as against the previous one.

A CONTINENT IN ARMS
The Armies of Europe on the Eve of World War I

By 1914 mass armies and conscription were the norm in Europe, save only in Britain, which relied on a small, professional volunteer force. Armies were enormous. France, with about 40 million people, maintained 605,000 men on active duty, mostly in the army. Some idea of the magnitude of this force—1.52% of the population—can be gained by noting that the combined strength of the active and reserve components of the American armed forces in the 1980s is less than 1.4% of the population: using the French ratio the U.S. would have active forces of 3,650,000 men. Moreover, in addition to active forces of great size, most armies maintained truly enormous reserve components. When France mobilized in 1914 she put roughly 4,000,000 men under arms, all trained and equipped, about 10% of the population. This is the equivalent in current American terms of 24,000,000 men, a figure which could not be attained in less than two years. Of course, France's effort was prodigious. Most other powers made do with armies statistically smaller. Austria-Hungary, for example, had only about 0.7% of her people under arms in peacetime, Russia but 0.8%, and Germany about 1%. But these countries were more populous than was France. The French army had to be prepared to meet the German army, yet Germany had roughly 50% more people than did France. So each year a greater proportion of Frenchmen served than did the citizens of any of the other major powers.

The accompanying table gives some idea of the combat strengths of the armies of the European

powers at the outbreak of World War I, 30 days after mobilization orders were issued. It should be noted that in most armies combat strength was only about 50% of mobilization strength, so the accompanying figures should be doubled to get some idea of total army strength, and then some allowance must be made for naval personnel. Within a year these forces would be considered small.

Notes: This table indicates the field strength of the powers, in both manpower and organized divisions and separate brigades. Letters in the right hand column refer to the accompanying notes.

A. Albania, created in 1913, had no real army by 1914. Figures are an estimate of available tribal levies and local forces.

B. Three fortress commands included as infantry divisions.

C. Figures include the Indian Army, which totaled five infantry and two cavalry divisions, all stationed in India, but exclude the relatively small forces maintained by the Commonwealth. Forces from the Commonwealth would not become available until the end of 1914, when elements of the untrained [1st] Canadian Division arrived in Britain.

D. Figures include four divisions and one brigade of infantry mobilized in North Africa for service in France.

E. Four of the infantry divisions were in Libya.

F. Figures exclude the East Indian Army.

G. Figures exclude the African Army.

H. Precise figures are impossible to obtain or estimate with any degree of confidence.

I. Considerable forces were being maintained in Morocco at this time.

J. Officially, combat strength was about double the figure given.

POWER	COMBATANTS (thousands)	FIELD FORMATIONS				NOTES
		Infantry		*Cavalry*		
		Div	Bdes	Divs	Bdes	
Albania	c. 60.0					A
Aust-Hung	1338.0	49	5	10		
Belgium	160.0	9		1		B
Britain	250.0	11	1	3	1	C
Bulgaria	300.0	12	7	1	1	
Denmark	85.0	3	1			
France	1800.0	85	5	10	1	D
Germany	2147.0	89	27	11		
Greece	150.0	8		1		
Italy	916.3	35		4		E
Montenegro	c. 60.0		11			
Netherlands	100.0	6			1	F
Norway	70.0		7			
Portugal	150.0	6			2	G
Romania	300.0	15	1	2	5	
Russia	c. 2500.0	114	?	36	?	H
Serbia	250.0	12	3	1		
Spain	300.0	14	3	1	3	I
Sweden	200.0	6		1		
Switzerland	250.0	6		4		
Turkey	400.0	36		4		J

Belgian General Leman, the defender of Liege.

On the night of 4-5 August, Emmich launched an attack with five infantry columns. Only one of the columns was successful. The *14th Brigade* slipped between two of the forts to capture the city of Liege on the morning of 7 August. This success was due to the resolution and bravery of a senior staff officer of the *Second Army*, *Generalmajor* Erich Ludendorff. The loss of the city made the Belgian Staff uneasy about the survivability of the ring of forts which surrounded it, and they promptly withdrew the 3rd Division behind the Gette River. The fate of the forts was sealed when a battery of Austrian 305mm siege howitzers arrived; they were slowly pulverized, the last falling on 16 August. Leman was captured unconscious in the rubble of his command post. By this time the bulk of two German armies had passed through to the west.

Brialmont fort of pentagonal shape.

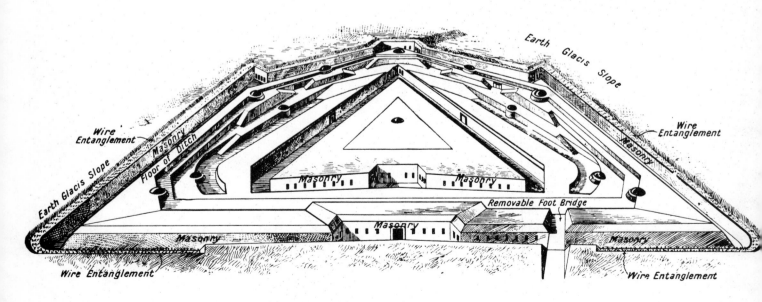

Brialmont fort of triangular shape.

Germans march through Liege.

KEY
Germans

OPENING MOVES INVOLVING GERMANY

KEY
Allies

1
NETH.
GERMANY
DEFENSIVE
RUSSIA
PLAN
BELG.
major
ATTACKS
minor
Paris
LUX.
FRANCE
AUSTRIA-HUNGARY

2
BRITAIN
NETH.
GERMANY
RAPID MOBILISATION
RUSSIA
AID
BEL.
FRANCE
APPEAL FOR DIVERSIONARY ACTION
AUSTRIA-HUNGARY

3
Antwerp ★ DELAY
NETH.
BELGIUM
GERMANY
FRANCE
Liège DELAY
Maubeuge ★ DELAY
Namur DELAY
LUX.
FIRST ARMY
to Paris
DIVERGING
SECOND ARMY
FRANCE

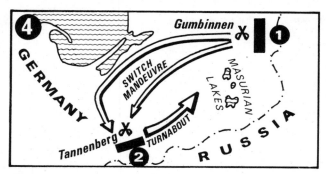

4
Gumbinnen
GERMANY
SWITCH MANOEUVRE
MASURIAN LAKES
Tannenberg
TURNABOUT
RUSSIA

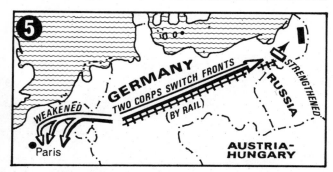

5
GERMANY
TWO CORPS SWITCH FRONTS
(BY RAIL)
STRENGTHENED
RUSSIA
WEAKENED
Paris
AUSTRIA-HUNGARY

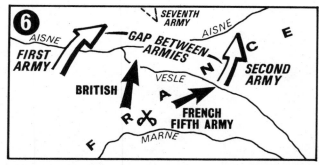

6
SEVENTH ARMY
AISNE
AISNE
FIRST ARMY
GAP BETWEEN ARMIES
VESLE
SECOND ARMY
BRITISH
FRENCH FIFTH ARMY
MARNE
FRANCE

7
Kovno
Vilna
★ Königsberg
RUSSIAN
FIRST
ARMY
GERMANY
EIGHTH ARMY
Masurian Lakes
Niemen
Grodno
RUSSIA

8
Lys
BELGIUM
B.E.F. Belgians
FRANCE
LUX.
Somme
FRENCH
Oise
AISNE

© Arthur Banks

These sections depict basic military moves involving Germany in the first weeks of the European campaign and illustrate how events and situations on her western and eastern fronts affected and reacted upon each other. In brief, her overall effort was split and she rapidly became involved in an active two-front war situation, the very position for which her detailed pre-war plans had been designed to avoid.

As the Germans broke into Liege, the Belgian Field Army drew up into positions behind the river Gette. They deployed five divisions between Diest and Perwez. Three were put in forward positions, the 2nd, 1st, and 3rd, with the 6th and 5th positioned as a reserve towards Namur. Namur, also fortified by Brialmont, was strongly garrisoned by fortress troops and the 4th Division. In effect the Field Army was masking the capital, Brussels. The strategic plan was to withdraw gradually past the capital, to retire northwestwards towards the Fortress of Antwerp and there to make a stand. The agony of Liege bought the time needed to deploy.

The Namur fortresses as seen from the river.

Namur

Skoda 30cm howitzer, transported across half of Europe to reduce the Belgian fortresses. Note the Austrian gunners.

The Adolf Bridge, Luxemburg. The Grand Duchess, Commander in Chief, and Minister of State of Luxemburg tried to halt the German advance here with three motor cars.

On 18 August *Generalobeust* Alexander von Kluck of the German *First Army*, 260,000 men strong, ordered an attack on the Gette line, to ease the Belgian Army away from Antwerp by outflanking them and driving them south. Despite von Kluck's efforts, the Belgian Army would not let itself be cut off. The Belgians fell back, abandoning Brussels on 20 August. Meanwhile, on 19 August the German *Second Army* under *Generalobeust* Karl von Bulow attacked the fortress of Namur, ringed by nine of Brialmont's forts mounting a total of 350 guns. By 21 August the Germans had brought up their 305mm Austrian Skoda howitzers and their new 420mm Krupps, the latter nick-named "Emma" and "Bertha." Three forts were destroyed on 22 August. Despite a vigorous Bel-

Bridge at Liege blown up to slow German advance. The Germans managed to capture most bridges intact.

gian counterattack, by 23 August only three forts remained. Pressed on all fronts the Belgian Army fell back on Antwerp in full retreat, while the 4th Division fled south towards the French lines. On 25 August Namur fell to the Germans.

Despite determined resistance, neither the Belgian Army nor the Belgian forts had played a decisive role. The German Army was not denied its strategic objectives. France was flanked, the four tracked Cologne-Liege-Paris railroad bridge over the Meuse and the railroad tunnel east of Liege were taken intact, and the Schlieffen Plan was unfolding.

THE IMPERIAL GERMAN ARMY IN 1914

The Kaiser on maneuvers. The photograph clearly reflects his active interest in military affairs.

The military situation in Germany was somewhat different than that in France. The level of civilian control was slight, mainly restricted to matters of budget. The Chancellor was not privy to any military planning nor was he consulted as a political advisor. All matters of doctrine and planning were left to the General Staff. Though the Kaiser was by constitutional mandate Commander-in-Chief and Supreme War Lord, he was given copies of war plans for review, but not for approval. Since in military affairs Kaiser Wilhelm II, had the knowledge of a competent platoon commander this was militarily not a bad idea. But politically it was disastrous. The real power lay in the hands of the Chief-of-the-General Staff.

While the pre-war army did not have a Grandmaison School to deal with, this does not mean that there was no debate in the army concerning the conduct of tactics and operations. The recent wars in South Africa and in Manchuria were observed and debated in the service journals. Many officers believed in aggressive tactics, and in this respect they were of a similar mind to the French. They held that the main enemy had to be overwhelmed as quickly as possible. This was, in essence, German strategy. As a result, in wartime the army was organized and deployed to accomplish this task on a front running from Hannover to Switzerland.

By 1913 the peace-time strength of the Imperial Army was 880,000 men, deployed in eight armies comprising 25 active army corps, totalling 50 active divisions. Upon mobilization the field armies

German Uhlans in a pre-war review. The lance was the Uhlans' distinctive weapon, but most German cavalry units were armed with it by 1914.

grew to 1,750,000, over 85% of, whom were to fight the French Army. Many of the supplementary first line troops were reservists. The operational plans called for the extensive use of reserve forces, both as individuals and whole units. The French Army did not place much confidence in their own reserve troops and as a result tended not to count them in the German order of battle either, a massive intelligence failure on their part.

The German cavalry division counted 5,200 men, twelve field guns, and six machineguns. These units practiced dismounted tactics and were trained to attack enemy positions and strong points on foot. This was a commendable role for cavalry, to act as mounted infantry, but the basic firearm they employed was unsuited to an infantry role. The German carbine had a range inferior to that of the standard infantry rifle, the Mauser '98. As a result, the cavalry tended to suffer from infantry fire while being unable to respond. In many units the lance was carried in addition to the sword and carbine.

The German infantry division numbered 17,500 men, 72 guns, and 24 machineguns. Trained to be

Spandau as it appeared in 1914. The German war chest was stored here.

aggressive, the German infantry could attack frontally, on the flanks, or by infiltration. They were well schooled in the use of small arms and particularly adept in indirect machinegun fire. The artillery closely supported the infantry in pressing the attack. If an attack failed they were to hold off any enemy counter-attack, while their own infantry reorganized. As soon as they regrouped, the German infantry was to go over to the attack once more and do this until they won.

The most significant advantage the Germans enjoyed was in the area of medium and heavy artillery. The Germans invested considerable time and resources in their medium and heavy guns. Not only did they have the 105mm field gun, they also had the 155mm howitzer. These were to prove to be a deadly combination. The 105mm field gun outranged the French 75mm—roughly equal to the German 77mm—leaving their infantry to be dispersed before it could press an attack. The 155 howitzer could

The standard German 77mm field gun. Artillerists wore a rounded version of the spike on their helmets.

attack both the French infantry and their artillery, which were exposed to barrages and counter-battery fire at great ranges. The Germans also had some very heavy guns, and the Belgian fortresses were pounded into dust by German 420mm howitzers and Austrian 305mm howitzers. In the areas of armaments, organization, and manpower the Germans had an almost decisive advantage over the Allied Forces.

German infantry firing.

Alsace-Lorraine

When, on 3 August 1914, Germany declared war on France, the French commander-in-chief designate Joseph Joffre summoned all five army commanders to his office at the Boulevard St. Germain. At 1600 hours he personally briefed them on the outlines of Case II of Plan 17. Joffre presented a very ambitious series of operational plans. France would take the initiative and attack very quickly. It would be a two-pronged blow force with each part pressing into German Lorraine, one above and one below the area of Metz-Thionville. The first offensive would be launched between the Vosges Mountains and the Moselle River, while a second was to be north of the line Verdun-Toul.

On 5 August Joffre moved his headquarters, the Great General Staff (GQG), to Vitry-Le-Francois. GQG consisted of Joffre as Commander-in-Chief, his deputy, or *Major General*, General-of-Division (Gen. Div.) Belin, and his chief-of-staff-*Aide-Major General*-Gen. Div. Henri Berthelot, each with their respective staffs, for a total of 92 officers and 534 men, a very small number to run such a large campaign.

Joffre with Castlenan and Pau. The aide at right has the new cloth cover for the red kepi.

Even before the troops began to march the French Army had made a series of critical errors in intelligence. Though Joffre confidently looked to the future, for the French had speedily and successfully deployed 1,071,000 men, he had no idea that Moltke was already across the Belgian frontier with some 840,000 men, the combined strength of four field armies, and that a further half-million were about to march. The Germans had stolen a march on the French and concentrated a significant superiority in manpower. France had 21 active army corps in the first line and did not envision a role for their reserve divisions other than keeping them in the second line, while the German Army fielded 22 active army corps plus a further 14 reserve corps in their first line.

According to Plan 17, the French offensive into Germany was to begin 13 days after mobilization, which in the event was 14 August. Plan 17 called for the French Right Wing to attack in the direction of Sarrebourg and Morlange. By 5 August, however, Joffre was growing impatient for some movement. On the 7th he ordered Gen. Auguste Dubail's First Army to send Bonneau's *VII Corps*, part of the covering force, into

General Pau

German-held Alsace.
  Bonneaus' command—the 14th and 41st

Reservists leave Paris. The red trousers dated from 1829, when they were adopted to provide a market for Algerian madder dyes.

Divisions and the 27th Infantry Brigade—was to capture Mulhouse, destroy nearby bridges over the Rhine, and then stir the Francophile populace into the revolt. Dubail added the 8th Cavalry Division and another infantry brigade from the Belfort Garrison, to bolster Bonneau's force. However, before he could move, Bonneau observed large German troop concentrations forming in Alsace between Fribourg and Keuzingen. Despite this, Bonneau was ordered to move on 7 August.

Bonneau took Altkirch after fierce fighting on 7 August, in an action which taught the need for closer cooperation between cavalry and in-

Belgian soldiers defend a bridge.

fantry. Though his troops were elated at liberating this 'last' bit of France, Bonneau was not pleased by his success; the Germans had not seemed surprised and appeared to have performed a planned withdrawal.

Despite Bonneau's misgivings, both Dubail and Joffre thought he was proceeding too slowly. On 8 August French troops entered Mulhouse, for the first time since 1870. The Germans, however, still held the Hardt Forest, east of the town. Bonneau requested time to rest his troops, but Dubail ordered an immediate attack. The French troops went into the forest. By 9 August German resistance had stiffened. Then, unexpectedly, the German *29th Division*

French artillery and dragoons.

counterattacked. French artillery halted the attack of the German *58th* and *84th Brigades*, and the situation was momentarily in doubt. However, *General der Infanterie* Freiherr von Heune of the German *XIV Corps* intervened to prevent a retreat. He ordered a renewed attack. Bonneau was forced to evacuate Mulhouse under German pressure. On 10 August Bonneau attempted a counterattack, but was forced to withdraw to avoid being enveloped.

After the initial stages of Plan 17, Joffre decided to modify the army's organization. On 11 August he created the Army of Alsace, under the popular, one-armed veteran of 1870 Gen. Paul Pau. Composed of the VII Corps, the 8th Cavalry Division, the 44th Division from Africa, the 1st Group of Reserve Divisions, the 57th Reserve Division from the Belfort Garrison, and five battalions of Chasseurs Alpins, this army was to cover the southern flank of the First Army. Joffre also created the Army of Lorraine under Gen. Michel Maunoury, entrusting him with the 64th, 65th, 67th, 74th, and 75th Reserve Divisions, to which the 54th, 55th, and 56th Reserve Divisions were later added. This army took up positions between the Second and Third Armies.

The creation of these additional armies helped solve some command problems, as the frontier armies were rather oversized. Unfortunately, Joffre created a few new problems of his own. His chief-of-staff sometimes removed units from commands without telling the army commanders of their action: Gen. Div. Pierre Ruffey of the Third Army found that a corps had been removed from his command without anyone informing him that the unit was no longer under his jurisdiction.

While Joffre was attacking in Alsace-Lorraine, the Germans were rolling back the Belgians. The news from Belgium did not cause alarm at Joffre's headquarters. The French greatly underestimated the capacity of the German forces. Having no confidence in reserve troops, they assumed that no one would use them as boldly as the Germans actually did. French intelligence estimates did not realize that the German Army was considerably larger than had been originally thought. Despite the fears expressed by Fifth Army commander Gen. Charles Lanrezac, G.Q.G. felt no sense of urgency about the security of the Ardennes and the Belgian frontier. Their opinions soon changed.

THE SCHLIEFFEN PLAN: AN ANALYSIS

Alfred von Schlieffen's sweeping plan for victory in a war with France has been a source of controversy almost from when it was conceived. Aside from Schlieffen's cavalier treatment of Germany's political leadership, his cavalier disregard for Germany's treaty obligations concerning Belgian neutrality, and his inept reading of the international political climate, one of the most important controversies revolves around the question of whether the plan, as originally conceived, was workable, and, if so, whether the Younger Helmuth von Moltke's alterations to the Schlieffen's original dispositions were fatal to its chances.

The Schlieffen Plan grew out of the failure of the German government to sustain close ties with Russia. As a result in 1892, Germany was confronted with the possibility of a two-front war. Helmuth von Moltke the Elder, former Chief-of-the-General Staff and architect of the Prussian victories over Austria in 1866 and France in 1870–1871, had speculated upon such a possibility and concluded that the best Germany could do would be to conduct a defensive war against France, while concentrating the bulk of her armies for a series of offensives against Russia in cooperation with Austria. He did not, however, believe it would be possible to strike a decisive knockout blow, but rather that such a conflict would be a lengthy one and preferably to be avoided.

Moltke's plan was essentially the one in force in 1891, when Schlieffen became Chief-of-the-General Staff in 1891. He found it unsatisfactory and began to speculate on the possibility of winning a major in a short, sharp campaign. He became infatuated with the Battle of Cannae, in 218 B.C., where Hannibal had succeeded in annihilating a Roman army twice the size of his own in a brilliantly executed double envelopment. From then until his retirement in 1905 Schlieffen devoted himself to the crafting of a plan which would permit Germany to smash France by means of a massive strategic envelopment of the French left, involving virtually all of Germany's mobile military strength. By his retirement the evolution of the plan had resulted in a number of politically explosive assumptions. To begin with was the "necessity" of violating Belgian and Netherlands neutrality in order to secure sufficient maneuver room for the massive wheeling movement envisioned. In addition, Schlieffen had welcomed an offer by the Italian General Staff to commit forces to his left flank so that he could increase the strength of his right still further. Ultimately, the final version of the plan envisioned placing 75% of Germany's total military power on the right flank in order to send it on a curving path through Belgium and into France so that by about the 39th day after mobilization the German armies would have enveloped the entire French army in the area between Paris and the German frontier. So obsessive had Schlieffen become with his grand vision that his final words are said to have been, "It must come to a fight, only keep the right wing strong!" But how realistic was this grand scheme? In retrospect, it must be admitted that Schlieffen's dream contained more than a small dose of wistful thinking.

Military plans usually contain a great many assumptions. In general, the more complex the plan, the more likely it is to fail. Schlieffen's plan was perhaps the most complex military plan in history, at once a mobilization plan, a deployment plan, and an operational plan. Each of these plans was meticulous. It required the troops on the outermost edge of the German right flank to sustain a daily rate of march in excess of 30 kilometers a day for nearly three weeks. In theory such a pace was possible, given certain assumptions. The principal assumption was that the Belgians would not actively resist the German advance, thus obviating the necessity of fighting them and permitting the capture of the Belgian railroads intact, so that the movement could be supported logistically. A second assumption was that the French would be so intent upon driving directly into Germany that would not recognize the danger to their rear until it was too late to matter. Finally, Schlieffen, unwilling to believe that Britain would intervene for the sake of what the Kaiser termed a "mere scrap of paper," suggested that even should such an eventuality arise, the "contemptible little army" would be swept up with the rest. Rarely mentioned in discussions of the plan is the fact that it was devised at a time when Russia, France's ally, was incapable of serious military action as a result of a monumental defeat in a war with Japan and consequent widespread internal upheaval. Schlieffen's plan was a magnificently detailed and complex formula for victory. In the event, of course, none of these assumptions proved valid. The Belgians did resist, bravely if not well, setting back Schlieffen's time-table by two or three days. Moreover, they managed to sabotage their rail system quite effectively—in one instance ramming 17 locomotives into each other in a critically important tunnel, causing a break-down in the movement of supplies to the troops. Indeed, had it not been for the season—high summer, with a bumper harvest just in—it is doubtful that the Germans would have gotten as far as they did. Nor, were the French quite so blind to reality as Schlieffen had hoped, so that they began to juggle forces about in order to confront the great German movement, using railroads to shift units more rapidly than could the foot-bound Germans. Then too, the British did intervene, and their army though admittedly little was hardly contemptible. And finally, by 1914 the Russians had achieved a considerable reorganiza-tion of their army and were intent upon striking in the East simultane-ous with the outbreak of war in the West, a matter which worried Moltke and East Prussian *junker* class, backbone of the German officer corps, a great deal more in practice than it did Schlieffen in theory. Schlieffen's magnificent plan began to come apart quite early in the campaign. As Napoleon had once said, "Unhappy the general who comes to the battlefield with a system."

Of course Schlieffen had many supporters in the German army and these enthusiastic followers refused to believe that the master's plan was flawed. Instead they blamed it on his successor, Helmuth von Moltke the Younger, who "tampered" with Schlieffen's inspired arrangements.

Moltke's reputation suffers from his failure as a commander. Neverthe-less, while no genius and certainly by no means a great general, he was a well-trained staff officer, with a great deal of experience and a realistic and practical attitude. A number of things about Schlieffen's tenure in command troubled him. Among his first decisions upon taking over was to prohibit the Kaiser from personally leading 60 squadrons of cavalry in a grand charge to conclude the annual maneuvers, a ridiculous practice which Schlieffen had permitted for years. More importantly, he found that he was uneasy with the great man's beautiful plan. There were too many things wrong. He began to tinker with it, ultimately placing more German troops on the left flank than Schlieffen had envi-sioned. This had the effect of raising the strength of the left wing from 11.1% of total German strength to 21.2%, with the result that the right wing fell from 75.0% to 67.5%. It is this action which has caused the most criticism of Moltke on the part of Schlieffen's enthusiastic acolytes. The refrain goes something like, "If only Moltke hadn't disturbed the balance between the two wings the plan would have succeeded." But was this actually the case?

In fact, while it is true that Moltke strengthened the left wing, he did not alter the ratio between the two wings. Indeed, in real terms he actually strengthened the right wing. There are a number of reasons for this. To begin with, by 1912 it was fairly evident that rising tensions between Italy and Austria-Hungary made an Italian presence on the Rhine highly unlikely. This removed ten infantry divisions from the order of battle, nearly 14% of the total envisioned for the Western

Front by the 1905 version of the plan. In addition, Moltke saw little reason to add the Netherlands to the list of Germany's enemies. Schlieffen had decided that the technical requirements of moving the armies required them to move across the so-called "Maastricht Appendix," the province of Lim-bourg, a little sliver of Dutch territory about 40 kilometers long and between seven and 24 kilome-ters wide, which dangles south from the mass of The Netherlands between Germany and Belgium. Moltke's analysis of the road net about Liege convinced him that it was possible to funnel both the *First* and the *Second Army* through the "Liege bottleneck." This obviated the necessity of fighting the Dutch, which would require two army corps. Furthermore, the increasing capability of German reserve forces permitted Moltke to substitute third-line *Landwehr* forces for the three corps which were ear-marked for the siege of Antwerp, to which the Belgians were expected to retreat after a token resistance. These economies saved ten divi-sions, precisely the number required on the left flank. Moltke did not shift these forces to replace the missing Italians, but left them on the right, so that the number of divisions on that flank was the same, 54, in both Schlieffen's original version of the plan and his modified one. He made the short-age of forces on the left flank by shifting one division from the Germany's already slender forces on the Eastern Front and by assigning to there divisions as they were formed. Thus, in the end the ratio of forces between the two flanks was somewhat superior to that established by Schlieffen in 1905, 3.6:1 as opposed to 3.2:1. More-over, since the forces originally earmarked for The Netherlands and Antwerp were now committed to the wheeling movement, operationally the ratio between the fronts was 3.8:1, about 18% greater than Schlieffen's original concept.

The accompanying tables summarize the technical details of the various versions of the Schlieffen Plan.

Tabular Summary of the Schlieffen Plan

Plan of 1905

Army		German	Italian	Combined
Divisions				
Total	(%)	72 (100.0)	10 (100.0)	82 (100.0)
East	(%)	10 (13.4)		10 (12.2)
West	(%)	62 (86.6)	10 (100.0)	72 (87.8)
Right	(%)	54 (75.0)		54 (65.8)
Left	(%)	8 (11.0)	10 (100.0)	18 (22.0)
Ratio R:L				4.0:1
Kms per Div				
Right				3.9
Left				11.7
Ratio R:L				0.33:1

Proposal of 1912

Army		German	Italian	Combined
Divisions				
Total	(%)	99 (100.0)	10 (100.0)	109 (100.0)
East	(%)	13 (13.1)		13 (12.0)
West	(%)	86 (86.9)	10 (100.0)	96 (88.1)
Right	(%)	75 (75.8)		75 (68.9)
Left	(%)	11 (11.1)	10 (100.0)	21 (19.2)
Ratio R:L				3.6:1
Kms per Div				
Right				2.8
Left				10.0
Ratio R:L				0.28:1

Proposal of 1914

Army		German	Italian	Combined
Divisions				
Total	(%)	80 (100.0)		80 (100.0)
East	(%)	9 (11.3)		9 (11.3)
West	(%)	81 (88.7)		81 (88.7)
Right	(%)	54 (67.5)		54 (67.5)
Left	(%)	17 (21.1)		17 (21.1)
Ratio R:L				3.9:1
Kms per Div				
Right				3.9
Left				12.4
Ratio R:L				0.31:1

These tables compare the three principal versions of the "Schlieffen Plan." The Plan of 1905 was that which Schlieffen left as a legacy to his successor, the Younger Moltke. The plan of 1914 was that which Moltke attempted to execute, after making various changes in Schlieffen's original arrangements. Critics of Moltke's arrangements invariably compare his dispositions in 1914 with those Schlieffen outlined for German forces alone in 1905, thereby totally ignoring the Italian contingent. Note, however, that when comparing the deployment figures for the combined German and Italian forces under the 1905 plan with the figures for the German forces alone in the 1914 version, Moltke has actually maintained the strength of the right wing at the same 54 divisions which Schlieffen had assigned, though as a proportion of the total German forces this wing fell from 75% to 67.5%. He did this despite the necessity of having to compensate for the absence of the Italians on his left wing. He managed this by allocating to that wing all divisions raised after 1905, and by deducting one division each from the left wing and to the Eastern Front, thus increasing somewhat the length of front which the divisions there would have to secure. Moreover, since Moltke decided against an invasion of The Netherlands—a telling power, that, for a military chief to make the essentially political decisions as to who would and who would not be invaded—and assigned third line forces to the siege of Antwerp, the active and reserve units originally committed to these operations he may be said to have actually increased the right wing by ten divisions, since originally only 44 were to make the great wheeling maneuver which was at the heart of the plan, so in a sense he actually increased strength on the right wing by about 22%.

Footnote: The Plan of 1912

The original version of the Schlieffen Plan, that of 1905 was rooted in German resources. However, the strategic problem presented by a war with both France and Russia continued to obsess Schlieffen in retirement. In addition, he began to notice Moltke's increasing unhappiness with the plan. As a result, in 1912 he developed a radically modified version of the plan which he embodied in a privately circulated memorandum. This proposal was for nothing less than a major reorganization and expansion of the German army. The active and reserve forces were to be merged into 51 oversized, new-style divisions, each with about 83% of the manpower of the old army corps. More importantly, the new divisions would have 87% of the manpower and 71% of the artillery of the French army corps, as well as 50% more machine guns. Operationally these would be the equivalent of 85 of the old style divisions, 42.5 corps. But not even this force was enough for Schlief-

fen, who seems to have been unhinged on the subject. He recommended the expansion of the army by a third, so that when "*Der Tag*—The Day" arrived, Germany would have the equivalent of 99 of the old-style divisions at hand, 49.5 army corps equivalents. Needless to say such an expansion was completely beyond the ability of the German economy to support, at least in peace time. Moreover, it would have seriously altered the social fabric of the German army: in that same year the high command rejected the formation of three additional corps—roughly seven of the new divisions—due to a shortage of aristocrats from which to recruit officers for them.

Key: Only infantry divisions have been counted. Percentage figures are always taken from the total of divisions available at the top of each table. *East* refers to Eastern Front, while *West* is the Western Front, which is divided into a *Right Wing*, the German *First*, *Second*, *Third*, *Fourth*, and

Fifth Army, and a *Left Wing*, the German *Sixth* and *Seventh* and the Italian *Third Army*. *Ratio* refers to the number of divisions on the right wing for each division on the left wing. *Kms per Div* is the number of kilometers of front for each division (the frontage of both the right and left wing was roughly 210 kilometers), with an indication of the ratio between the two.

THE FRENCH ARMY IN 1914

The French service regulations stated that the infantry was the primary arm of combat. Morale and training were considered of the utmost importance in preparing the infantry for this role. The French soldier had to be thoroughly trained in order to offset the German superiority in manpower. This concern for training was one of the reasons given by the army for restoring three year conscript service in 1913. Three regulations concerning troop formations were published during the years 1913–1914. The influence of the Grandmaison school was in evidence, as commanders were urged to commit their forces at the earliest moment after encountering the foe, even if advanced guards had made no previous reconnaissance or contact with the enemy. Emphasis was placed on rapidity of marching, of maneuver, and of concentration.

The French Army which entered the war in August of 1914 was wedded to the offensive both in strategy and in tactics. Of course, the spirit of the offensive was a moving force in the plans and the doctrines of the British Army, the German Army, and the Russian Army, so, the French are not unusual in this respect. They were more offensive-minded than the others. The term *offensive á outránce* was used to describe the aggressive tactics of the French infantry. The General Staff used this doctrine to formulate Plan 17, the offensive against the German-held provinces of Alsace-Lorraine and against Southern Germany.

The adoption of such a strategy and such tactics was the result of 40 years of studying the reasons for the defeat of the French Imperial Army in the Franco-Prussian War of 1870–71. French military writers believed that the underlying cause of that defeat was the defensive mindedness of the army, a lack of offensive spirit. The infantry had fought from defensive positions, only to be outflanked by Prussian infantry or pounded off the field by

The famous French "75" with its ammunition limber.

superior Prussian artillery. The enemy had acted with speed and initiative, while the French lost all tactical and strategical momentum.

In the decade before the First World War, an offensive school of thought grew up inside the French Army, greatly influenced by the articles and lectures of Col. Louis Loizeau de Grandmaison. Grandmaison's ideas found acceptance at all levels in the army, ranging from company commanders up to generals Foch and Joffre. Modern writers have tended to dismiss this doctrine of the offensive as simpleminded fanaticism. However, this is not necessarily true, particularly if one examines the basic principles of the doctrine.

French troops at Champagne. The carefully arranged, but heavy, loads carried by French soldiers are shown to good advantage.

French infantry moves past German barbed-wire.

French machine gun section on the march

This doctrine was quite remarkable considering that the average French infantryman carried between 80 and 90 pounds of field gear, equipment, and ammunition. In addition, he carried the Model 1886/M92 8mm Lebel Rifle, a long, cumbersome, and inefficient weapon. The French infantryman's uniform was also unique, comprising a red kepi, blue overcoat, and red trousers, at a time when the rest of Europe had adopted, or started to adopt, khaki or grey field uniforms. During the decade prior to 1914, the French army had actually tried to introduce a modern uniform. Despite legend, only a minority of the officers had opposed this idea. The new uniform was defeated by the National Assembly and budgetary considerations, not by idiotic militarists: the old uniform was considered to be the symbol of Republican virtue by a great many politicians and newspaper editors.

The followers of the offensive had an additional tool, the 75mm Model 1897 field gun. This weapon could hurl a 16 pound shell 7,500 yards, and a trained crew could sustain a fire of between six and seven rounds a minute, with 20 as a theoretical maximum. The doctrine of the French artillery was also to engage the enemy as quickly as possible. In theory, the enemy would be smothered by artillery fire and attacked with great speed by the infantry before he could deploy his own forces. Decisive command, speed, and morale would prevail.

French 75mm guns in action

French infantry bring up supplies. The soon-to-be-famous "poilu" beard is beginning to make an appearance.

storm raised doubts about offensive tactics all over Europe.

Nevertheless, despite rising doubt and increasing criticism, the offensive school had an advantage. The war plan against Germany was Plan 17, the attack eastwards into Southern Germany. The Vice-President of the Supreme War Council, Maj. Gen. Joseph Joffre was a supporter of both aggressive tactics and aggressive strategy. As the Commander-in-Chief designate in the event of war, he enjoyed the confidence of the War Minister and a sizeable following inside the French General Staff. Since Napoleon, no soldier in France had possessed such authority inside the army. Thus the French Army would enter the war wedded to its doctrine.

However, not everyone inside the army saw matters in this light. The offensive was meeting with resistance at the Supreme War College. Two respected officers there criticized Grandmaison's ideas, Col. Henri Petain, a future Marshal of France, and Col. the Count de Maud'huy, later commander of the XVIII Corps. They were joined by Maj. Gen. Charles Lanrezac, the commander-designate of the Fifth Army, and a member of the Supreme War Council. A number of officers observed that since the 1880s weapons had become more lethal. The killing range of the infantryman's rifle had increased three-fold since the adoption of smokeless powder. The artillery's possibilities were now limitless, with recoiling barrels and new shells, so that guns were far deadlier than anything known in the previous century. And, perhaps most importantly, the machinegun had finally come into its own during the Russo-Japanese War in Manchuria (1904–1905). As Petain stated in his lectures on the nature of firepower, even the most determined assault could be stopped and broken by any combination of rifle, machinegun, and artillery fire. The slaughter of the Japanese infantry as they tried to take Port Arthur by

Crowd in Paris waits for news from the front.

French Cuirassier poses with carbine. In fact, these troops had little training in dismounted actions.

French stretcher teams working by searchlight. The light throws into contrast the men's blue-grey overcoats and the officer's blue-black tunic.

Prior to a declaration of war, the highest permanent formation in the French Army was the corps. Army commanders-designate held a letter of appointment for one year, which could be renewed by the War Minister. The army commanders reviewed their prospective areas of operations and their troops as inspectors during annual maneuvers. This peculiar tenure of office made effective leadership difficult. General officers and their staffs had but a limited time to familiarize themselves with their troops, the terrain, and intelligence concerning potential enemy movements.

The prewar strength of the French Army consisted of 33,600 officers and 601,500 other ranks, a total of 635,000 men. Of these, approximately 150,000 were overseas or on special duties, leaving some 450,000 regulars available for duty in France. On mobilization, which was proclaimed at 1600 hours on 4 August 1914, the active troops deployed on the frontier to guard against any sudden German attack. Meanwhile the call went out for a general mobilization of 27 year classes totalling 3.5 million men. The first men to be called were the combat troops of the three most recently serving classes, 1911, 1912, and 1913. They completed their mobilization in five days, filling out the combat units. The next group called up were support troops. The field forces consisted of 29 corps of two divisions and one army corps of three divisions. This gave Joffre over 940,000 men to use in the offensive. The remaining 2,640,000 were reserve or second line personnel. Unlike the Germans, the French did not expect to use reserve units in Plan 17. The French Army did not devote a great deal of time or effort in bringing their reserve divisions up to regular

French light cavalry receiving mail. Their tunics and shell jackets are sky-blue, much lighter than those worn by infantry.

standards: The reserves are zero, expressed the professional's opinion perfectly. In France the reserve officer or noncommissioned officer obtained no social benefit or preference in government service as a result of their status.

The basic maneuver unit of the

rifle used by the infantry. The *cyclistes* were really infantrymen and were supposed to accompany the cavalry into action and provide protection from hostile infantry, for French cavalrymen were not trained for dismounted combat.

The backbone of the French army was the infantry. The infantry division, consisting of 15,000 men, 36 guns, and 24 machineguns in two brigades of two regiments, each of three battalions, was the main arm of maneuver and attack.

While French infantry equipment was generally similar to Germany's, neither the French rifle nor their machinegun were as modern as their German counterparts. The reliance on the 75mm gun limited the training in small arms markmanship. Despite these significant technological disadvantages the French army would withstand the shock of initial defeat and turn the tide to victory.

German flags captured by the French. Most European armies had stopped carrying colors in battle, but the Germans still did, especially on the Eastern Front.

French army was the division. There were two types of divisions, cavalry and infantry.

The cavalry was armed and trained for mounted combat, with virtually all regiments carrying the lance. The only exception to this rule were the *cuirassiers*, heavy cavalry men who wore an armored breastplate. Cavalry performed its traditional roles of reconnaissance and screening the movement of armies. It could seize bridges and railways and pursue a defeated enemy. A French calvary division numbered 4,500 men and eight guns. Tactically it consisted of three cavalry brigades and one horse artillery brigade, of two batteries, plus a *groupe cycliste* of four officers and 320 other ranks. The average cavalryman was armed with the Model 1890 carbine and a saber. The range of the carbine was less than a third that of the Lebel

Zouaves on the march.

German artillery in temporary concealment. Red
unit numbers were often worn on the cloth helmet
covers.

CHAPTER II

THE BATTLES OF THE FRONTIERS

THE initial skirmishing had been indecisive. But little more than a week after the war began, a series of battles erupted along the Franco-German frontier and in Belgium, as the main strength of the opposing armies clashed for the first time. Known collectively as the "Battles of the Frontier," these engagements were critically important in shaping the course of the war.

Alsace

Bonneau's VII Corps of the First Army, which had so gloriously raised the 'tricoleur' in Alsace after over 40 years of German rule, was quickly forced out of Mulhouse and by 12 August was back in the Belfort area. However, Pau's newly formed Army of Alsace soon renewed the attack on Mulhouse. The Germans started to concentrate their forces to counter expected French movements in the Alsace-Lorraine, but kept only three brigades as a covering force in Upper Alsace. Between 14 August through 19 August the French began a series of attacks. Their initial advance saw Pau reoccupy Mulhouse and he was soon also in possession of Altkirch and Munster Worth. The hilly, broken terrain of this region aided the defense. The retreating Germans made effective use of machineguns and camouflaged artillery, using aircraft to spot for their artillery. As a result, the French were frequently forced to ground when they walked into ambushes.

Lorraine

In Lorraine, a vigorous offensive by the French First Army, under Dubail, threw *Generalleutnat* Josias von Heeingen's German *Seventh Army* back towards Strasbourg and Lower Alsace, in an offensive which relied on the cooperation with elements of Gen. Dir. Noel de Castelnau's Second Army. However, the French advance was soon slowed by a combination of terrain and German tactics. Their VIII Corps was stopped outside Sarrebourg and at Doming and Gosselmig, as the French infantry suffered greatly at the hands of accurate German artillery fire, but in general the First Army gained ground.

By 13 August, Dubail's First Army had two corps across the Meurthe River. The XII and VIII Corps advanced on 14 August and by the 15th took the towns of Cirey and Balmont, pushing the *I Bavarian Corps* back to the vicinity of Sarrebourg.

By the evening of 17 August, the two French troops had established a line stretching from Vasperller-Hepach-St. Georges and the XXI Corps extended the line toward the Vosges. On 18 August, the II Cavalry Corps advanced on Sarrebourg, which it entered after a brief skirmish. The XII Corps then moved northeast to Walschied, while the XII Corps held the heights north and east of Sarrebourg and the VIII Corps moved on Heming, seized the passage of the Marne-Rhine Canal, and entered Sarrebourg. By 19 August the First Army had reached the line of La Pontraye-St. Marie aux Mines-Schirmeck-Sarrebourg. Plan 17 seemed to be working. Then the situation changed.

On 20 August the German *Sixth Army*, under Crown Prince Rupprecht of Bavaria, counterattacked. Five German army corps struck the VIII Corps on the French right flank.

King George V. Although Britain's constitutional monarchy limited his direct role, he and the Royal Family were a great moral example throughout the war.

Prince Rupprecht of Bavaria.

Chow time for German troops in Brussels.

Kiel, German port with access to the North Atlantic, closely monitored by the British throughout the war.

General Maud'huy

Reacting quickly to Rupprecht's attack, Dubail moved his reserves, sending two brigades through his left flank in a night march to take the bridges at Sarre, Gosselming, and Oben Stinzel. If this movement had been successful, an opening would have been made into the German rear for his cavalry. After intense fighting the French infantry took Gosselming by bayonet assault. The Germans promptly counterattacked and an infantry assault supported by artillery drove the French out of the town.

The French center and right were more fortunate. Their XXI Corps had met no resistance since 19 August, when it stopped an attack by the German *XIV Corps* near Walscheit, and the XIII Corps had not yet been engaged. The XIII was brought into the line and attacked to the northeast of Sarrebourg, helping to disengage the right flank of the VIII Corps, which clung to the town until nightfall. This permitted the 16th Division, which had fought with great skill and determination, to withdraw from the town.

It was as the French regrouped and continued their efforts to seize crossings across the Sarre Bridges, that five of Prince Rupprecht's corps struck VIII Corps, their left flank. Dubail had intended to entrench along the line Kerpich-Soldaten Kopf, consolidate, reorganize, and then to advance. The German attack soon cancelled any idea of continuing the offensive. On the morning of 21 August Dubail retreated towards Balmont. On 23 August the First Army held a front from Dames-Aux-Bois to Col du Bonhomme, with little to show for their efforts over the past few days. The army had suffered heavy casualties: VIII Corps alone lost 50% of its strength. Dubail soon learned that Noel de Castelnau's Second Army had suffered a similar disaster.

The French Second Army

On 14 August elements of the French Second Army advanced into German territory. The XVI and XV Corps moved in the direction of Avricourt with the bulk of the XX Corps, commanded by the widely regarded Ferdinand Foch, while the remainder of XX Corps screened the front towards the north. By evening the Second Army was facing to the northeast on the high ground of Gonrexon. Enemy resistance was substantial. On 15 August the XV Corps had been stopped at Moncourt by the Germans. Losses for the XV Corps had been heavy, however the XVI and XX Corps had made progress. The IX Corps stood on the Grand Couroune, east of Nancy, and had sent out screening detachments towards the northeast. Despite resistance, the French made progress.

By 16 August the French reached Morhouse as the Germans continued to retreat. On 17 August the Second Army moved northwest toward Delme-Chateau-Dieuze. The XVI Corps advanced without difficulty, while the XX Corps occupied Chateau Salius and conducted reconnaissance northwards, but the XV Corps, which managed to occupy Marsal, could not move beyond the Seille, as German resistance began to stiffen. The Germans had fallen back about as far as they were willing to go. Resistance began to stiffen.

On 18 August, the French XVI Corps was attacked by strong German forces. German artillery fire held up the XV Corps in the Seille Valley and prevented the occupation of Dieuze. The XVI Corps was forced back to Agnviller. Despite stiffening German resistance, the XX Corps managed to advance north of Morville-les-Vic and Chateau Salius. At this critical point, the IX Corps was transferred to the Fourth Army. Despite the loss of 20% of his army, de Castelnau ordered an attack in the direction of Loudrefing, Bensdorf, and Morthauge. It was the last gasp of Plan 17.

The Second Army's offensive was halted on 19 August: the XVI Corps was stopped along the Salines Canal, while XV Corps could not pass the towns of Zommange and Vergaville. The XX Corps did manage to advance, pushing a brigade to Morhange, with its left flank covered by the 68th Reserve Division, which came up to replace the IX Corps. On 20 August de Castelnau ordered an attack by XVI and XV Corps on the line of Cutting-Dommon-Bassing, while the XX Corps was to consolidate its positions and stand ready to move to the northeast. But France's moment had passed, the Germans were ready to hit back.

On 20 August the Germans went over to the offensive, throwing de Castelnau's left flank back on Chateau Salius. The right flank of the

Russia's ill-fated Czar Nicholas II. First cousin to both King George and Kaiser Wilhelm, his order for Russian mobilization in 1914 hastened the outbreak of war.

German infantry advancing. Despite modern weapons and uniforms, German units moved in packed, antiquated formations.

Zouave band on the eve of war. By 1914, these elite infantrymen were Frenchmen in exotic uniforms, not true North Africans.

Maurice Farman biplane. Initially an observer, the cockpit forward of the "pusher" propeller lent itself to machine-gun mounting.

French Second Army was thus cut off from Dubail's First Army. At 1600 hours de Castelnau ordered a retreat, which was to continue into 21 August. Despite the timely arrival of reinforcements—two reserve divisions and the II Cavalry Corps—the French were forced to retire west of the Meurthe, their left finally coming to rest on St. Nicholas. In the north, three divisions still held the Grand Couronne. Meanwhile, in his headquarters at Vitry-Le-Francois, Joffre was completely unaware of the retreat of de Castelnau's Army.

The German Crown Prince in the uniform of the 1st Death's Head Hussars which he wore throughout the war.

The Battle of the Meuse

Despite the reverses on his right, Joffre persisted in his belief in Plan 17. He ordered Ruffey's Third Army and Fernand de Langle de Cary's Fourth Army to attack into the Ardennes. Langle's Fourth Army was to strike through the Ardennes toward Neufchateau, its right flank guarded by the Third Army, which would move towards Arlon. The French high command was confident that this movement would be successful. Their intelligence staff had estimated that the German forces in the area totaled only six corps and three cavalry divisions, and Joffre was committing eight corps and three cavalry divisions to the attack against them. In fact, the French collided with the German *Third* and *Fourth Armies*. The French army commanders had been given instructions "to attack the enemy wherever met," and they did so. Joffre had created the Army of Lorraine

under Gen. Michel Joseph Maunroy, with orders to defend the Hauts de Meuse to support the advance of the Fourth and Third Army, moving to besiege Metz and Thionville. As this new army was made up of reserve divisions, the Fourth and Third Army could expect little help from it. However, as Joffre believed German strength to be minimal, he expected the French armies to advance with ease. In fact, he was wrong. Actual German strength was ten corps, two cavalry divisions, and six Landwher brigades, the bulk of the German *Fourth* and *Third* Armies. The French had grossly underestimated the German strength opposite the Third and Fourth Armies. Worse yet, on 21 August, the *Fifth Army*, under the Crown Prince Wilhelm of Prussia, was about to advance, and Wilhelm's cavalry was already observing the French movements towards the Ardennes.

French cavalrymen sleep on heaps of straw in a town square. Cavalry averaged two hours less sleep per night than infantry during the campaign.

Czar Nicholas and Kaiser Wilhelm in happier days pose before a Russian Guard unit.

On the evening of 21 August the Third Army arrived at the line Conz-Lagranville-Tellancourt-Virton. At Virton, elements of the army tried to establish communications with the right flank of the Fourth Army. On 22 August marching columns advanced through a dense fog, taking almost no precautions against the enemy. Ruffey's center, V Corps, collided with an enemy corps. The French fought with great fury. However, the fog lifted, exposing them and their artillery to the longer ranging German guns. On the right flank, Maurice Sarrails' VI Corps was attacked by three German corps. By 1100 hours Sarrail was barely holding on. Meanwhile Third Army's left flank, IV Corps, was attacked by two German corps. The corps began to crumble. Ruffey's Third Army was fighting for its life, three corps against six.

The defeat of Third Army's IV Corps at Virton threatened the right flank of the Fourth Army. The Germans now struck de Langles' XVII Corps. This too was crushed. The defeat of XVII Corps sealed the fate of this army. On 23 August both French armies retreated, not halting until the 25th. The right of the Fourth Army fell back between Chievs and the Meuse, while the Third Army retired to the Meuse. The situation became more critical when Third Army's IV Corps was once again defeated, at Marville, almost losing its artillery. The corps was only saved by the intervention of Fourth Army's II Corps. Aided by II Corps, newly arrived from Fifth Army, IV Corps retired across the Meuse.

While disaster was developing on his right, Joffre began to realize that the situation on his left and in Belgium was becoming critical. On 25 August he decided to reinforce the left of the Allied armies. The Army of Lorraine was dissolved. One group of reserve divisions was left to defend the Hauts-de-Meuse, while the 55th and 56th Divisions were taken by rail to Montdidier to form the nucleus of a new Sixth Army under Michel Maunroy. By 26 August the Fourth Army was on the left bank of the Meuse, with a cavalry screen connecting it to the Fifth Army, while its right flank was in contact with the Third Army. The badly battered Third Army took no further action in the battle of the Meuse.

German Jagers pass in review in Lourain.

French 27cm howitzer. French artillerists traditionally wore a less visible uniform of dark blue.

Regroupment

On 26 August, Joffre ordered the Fourth Army to fight a decisive battle on the Meuse. As German infantry units had already crossed the river, the French hoped to use a series of counterattacks to push them back across the Meuse before they could be supported by artillery. An attack by the Colonel Corps—tough regulars from North Africa—failed. The corps was driven back, its withdrawal halted only with the arrival of units from the II Corps. On the right flank, however, II Corps drove the Germans into the river at Cesse and Luzy, while on the left the French also drove the Germans back, as reinforced with two reserve divisions, the XI Corps defeated the Germans at La Marfee.

On 27 August, the Fourth Army commander, de Langle de Cary, gave an order to throw the Germans over the Meuse. Joffre, beginning to sense the magnitude of the disaster facing France, countermanded this and ordered a retirement to the Asine. The battle field was calm on August 28th. Despite having repulsed the German *Fourth Army*, the French Fourth Army was forced to retire. Meanwhile, although its earlier attacks had met with a lack of success, on 23 August the First Army started a three week offensive designed to stop the German attack in Alsace-Lorraine and to aid de Castelnau's Second Army, which was under extremely heavy attack. Though short of troops because the XXI Corps had been sent to take part in the Battle of the Meuse, the First Army began its attack on the 24th, even as de Castelnau threw the Germans back to the northeast. From 28 August through 31 August the Germans held Dubail's attacks, while their *Sixth* and *Seventh Armies* tried to force the Gap of Charmes, so they could carry out an enveloping movement to the west of the Vosges.

Fighting was heavy in the Grand Couronne and the Vosges during the last days of August. By the end of the month, the French right wing armies were being weakened by drafts for the new armies being created on their left. De Castelnau's Second Army, having lost the 18th Division and the XV Corps to Joffre's left, could not continue its offensive. The French attacks in Alsace-Lorraine had everywhere met defeat. The focus of operations was rapidly shifting to the northwest.

Henry Farman biplane, used for observation duties by both British and French early in the war.

The Queen of the Belgians.

French colonial troops recover German equipment from a battlefield.

THE ARMY CORPS

	Belg	Br	Fr Act	Fr Res	Ger Act	Ger Res	Neth	Rus	Swss
Manpower	25.5	40.0	45.0	47.4	44.0	38.0	23.3	32.0	30.0
Bayonets	19.8	24.0	28.3	39.6	28.0	28.8	19.5	25.6	21.6
Bns: Number	18	24	24	36	24	25	18	32	42
Men	1.1	1.0	1.2	1.1	1.17	1.15	1.08	0.8	0.51
MGs: Number	18	48	48	72	48	54	24	64	48
Ratio	0.9	2.0	1.7	1.8	1.7	1.9	1.2	2.5	2.2
Arty: Lt	48	118	126	162	108	72	36	96	96
Mdm	24	44	—	—	52	—	12	12	—
Ratio	2.8	6.8	4.8	4.1	5.7	2.5	2.1	4.2	4.5
Cav: Sqns	5	5	6	—	6	3	4	12	4
Men	0.6	0.53	0.9	—	0.72	0.36	0.48	1.8	0.6
MGs	1	2	2	—	—	—	—	2	—
Engr Coys	3	5	5	1	6	3	2	6	10
Sig Sects	3	6	8	1	6	3	2	4	6
Aircraft	—	4	4	—	4	—	—	4	—

Key: *Manpower*, the total number of troops in the corps, in thousands. *Bayonets*, the total number of officers and men equipped to fight as infantry, in thousands. *Bns*, the number of infantry battalions—usually grouped in brigades of six—along with the number of men. *MGS*, the number of machine guns in the corps, exclusive of those in the attached cavalry, with the ratio per thousand bayonets. *Arty* is the number of artillery pieces attached, divided into *Lt*, light (up to 77mm/18-pdr), and *Mdm*, medium (above 77mm/18-pdr), with the ratio of pieces per thousand bayonets. *Cav* is the number of cavalry squadrons attached, with strength in thousands and number of machine guns assigned to the cavalry. *Eng Coys*, the number of companies of engineers attached. *Sig Sects*, the number of sections of signal troops. *Aircraft* is the number at least theoretically assigned for reconnaissance purposes, which existed largely on paper in Russian corps.

=========================

In 1914 the standard operational organization of most armies was the army corps, usually of two infantry divisions plus supporting troops, though two French regular corps—IX and Colonial—and their "Groupes de Reserve," had three divisions each. This table outlines the basic strength of the army corps of the Western Front powers, with Russia thrown in for comparison and The Netherlands and Switzerland included in as much as initial German planning had postulated invasions of both. The French "Groupes de Reserve" have been included despite the fact that they were neither intended nor equipped for first line service. Soon after the campaign began the French reserve formations were taking their place in the front lines. The Belgian and Netherlands formations included in this table were not actually army corps (*corps d'armee*), but "divisions of the army" (*divisions d'armee*), large organizations with three or four infantry brigades, intermediate in size between the corps and divisional tables of organization favored by the major powers, which had been created for the sake of economy. Three such divisions which were theoretically the equal of two major power army corps. All figures are, in any case, "ideal." In all armies there were often units which did not conform to the normal tables of organization and equipment. While there was a high degree of standardization among the formations of the great powers, two Belgian divisions actually had 24 battalions, with other figures proportionately higher, while Swiss corps strength could vary between 28 and 42 battalions. In addition, the six battalions of reservists totalling 4,500 men theoretically attached to each French corps have been omitted, as

has the cavalry division usually
attached to each Russian corps.

THE BELGIAN ARMY IN 1914

The defense of Belgium rested on two foundations, her neutrality, guaranteed by the Treaty of London of 1839, and an extensive system of fortifications. Neither of these proved to be very effective. During the 1880s the Belgian government began the construction of a new type of fortification known as the Brialmont System. The forts were supposed to be mutually supporting and impervious to the heaviest siege artillery. This system was used in the defenses constructed at the cities of Liege, Namur, and Antwerp. In the event of invasion the Belgian Field Army was supposed to cover and support the fortified areas.

Unfortunately, the field army, the instrument that was to perform the function of active support, was not prepared to do so. Belgium had long before chosen to end its reliance on long serving professional soldiers and changed over to conscription. In 1909 the Belgian Army had begun to build a reservist force based on two years service. Due to low military budgets, the planned strength of the field forces, 150,000 men, had not been reached by 1914. As a result, when hostilities broke out actual field strength was about 117,000 men.

The Belgian Field Army had six "army" divisions and a cavalry division. The "army" division theoretically contained between 25,000 and 32,000 men, with 60 field pieces and 18 machineguns. The cavalry division was composed of 4,500 men and 12 field guns. The army could be supplemented by members of the Gendarmerie and the Civil Guard, an additional 25,000 lightly armed troops. Equipment of all arms was adequate, but Belgian tactics tended to reflect French thinking.

Organization of a Belgian division in 1914. Note how infantry, cavalry and artillery are integrated in a manner advanced for the times.

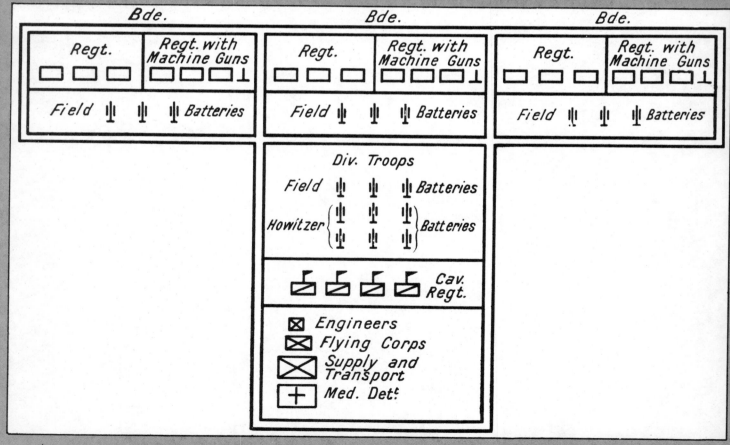

British wartime sketch of German shelling of Belgian emplacements.

Belgium was drawn into the war because the Germans wanted to make use of the Belgian railway network to take them to the northern border of France. The city of Namur was the meeting point of six railway lines. It was protected by 350 guns in the surrounding fortifications and was considered to be the pivot of any French invasion of Belgium. The French Supreme War Council in Paris had, in fact, discussed an invasion plan of Belgium in 1912. The President and the Cabinet had turned the plan down after consulting with the British Government, which gave a negative reply to any preemptive invasion. No such political review took place in Germany. The result was the German invasion.

The Belgian Army was hard pressed to develop an effective defense in August of 1914. Eastern Belgium was rapidly overrun by the Germans, the fortresses of Liege and Namur were quickly invested. On 16 August Liege fell, followed by Namur on 25 August. Despite spirited resistance on the Dyle, and a counterattack at Namur, the Belgian attempt to defend their country was unsuccessful. The Belgian Army was forced to retreat, first to Brussels, then to Antwerp, the last remaining great fortress. Since their construction during the late 1880s the Belgian fortifications had not been updated or reconstructed to withstand modern artillery. The forts proved to be highly vulnerable. The rapidity of

the German assault meant that the reinforcements who were to man the outer works failed to arrive. The forts did not support each other and were invested one by one. In the end, despite good courage and sacrifice, the Belgian Army would retain only a small foothold in its own country.

German Jagers captured by the British in Belgium.

Belgian infantry in 1914. Their blue-black uniforms were less visible than the French red and blue, but were replaced by a British-style khaki the following year.

Dunkirk in 1914. HQ for exiled Belgians.

THE BRITISH ARMY IN 1914:
The "Old Contemptibles"

Sir Ian Hamilton in the pre-war fall dress of the Black Watch. His activities in 1914 were overshadowed by his later command at Gallipoli.

Unlike her continental neighbors, Britain did not adopt conscription as the basis of her military system. As always, the long-serving regular remained the backbone of the British military system. The army was small and professional. In one sense this was a source of strength, but it was also a source of weakness. The strength came from the officer corps, which was selected from the upper classes. The standards for conduct were high. Since the officers were for the most part independent in means, their demands on the government were slight. The enlisted men were recruited primarily from the urban poor. If they survived the rigors of service they could look forward to a modest pension upon completion of twenty years in the ranks. The non-commissioned officers were seasoned veterans, as were most of the men.

The traditional strategy pursued by Britain up to the end of the nineteenth century was an insularity maintained by naval supremacy. The army was relegated to the defense of the colonial empire, with at least one half of its active strength in India alone. Forces in the home islands served as training and depot units. This system worked well so long as Britain's military commitments were limited. Nevertheless, the demands of almost simultaneous campaigns in the Sudan, South Africa, and India in the period 1896–1902 caused severe pressure on the manpower base of the army.

The South African War (1899–1902) started off disastrously for the British Army. In general, the performance of the army was lackluster. The opening campaign was typified by poor field craft. Many officers showed up with wagon loads of luggage. The average soldier could not shoot effectively, due to the fact that the annual ammunition allotment for target practice was less than 50 rounds. The field guns were out of date and lacked sufficient range for modern combat. The regular cavalry was trained for mounted combat only, armed with a carbine which made them no match for the Boer mounted infantry. In sum, at the onset of the twentieth century, the British Army was unprepared for modern war.

The decade that followed the South African War turned out to be eventful. It saw the creation of a General Staff, giving the army coordinated command and operational planning in peace time. Permanent army corps areas were created. As an initial, tentative understanding with France became more formal, a British Expeditionary Force was created. Thus, in the event of war, Britain would send two corps—four infantry divisions—and a cavalry division to the assistance of the French.

The tactical and organizational lessons of the South African War

Royal Flying Corps B.E.2s in Flanders.

Australian Victoria Mounted Rifles NCO and "mate."

were implemented in the decade that followed. A standard rifle was issued to both the infantry and the cavalry, making the British Army the only one in Europe to have a single shoulder arm. Standards in small arms training improved to the point that the British soldier was the best shot in Europe, able to put 20 rounds on target in a minute. Fieldcraft also improved. While in the field, officers were required to live simply and look after their men. The cavalry was trained in dismounted tactics. The artillery was completely modernized, with the Royal Horse Artillery receiving the 13-pounder gun, the field artillery, the 18-pounder and the 4.5 inch howitzer, and the heavy battalions, the 60-pounder, equalling anything in the German Army.

The prewar army was composed of approximately 250,000 men. With half the strength assigned overseas, the question of reserves became critical. The old system had failed during the South African War. The British Army lacked any organized reserves. Neither the Volunteers nor the Yoemanry were obliged to serve outside Britain. The Militia could only send those few who received a special overseas subsidy. The war effort in South Africa was kept going by a hodge-podge of drafts from the Militia, Volunteers coming into service as individuals, and Imperial Volunteers. The creation of the Territorial Force helped to correct this situation. Organized into permanent bodies drawn from a particular locality, much the same as regular regiments, the Territorials were to relieve the Regular Army in the defense of the British Isles. This arrangement made it possible to send another corps to France at the end of August in order to reinforce the B.E.F. On the outbreak of war in 1914, the strength of the Territorial Force stood at 140,000 men in six divisions.

London Scottish Rifle Volunteers in their distinctive "Hodden grey" kilts. Reservists of all combatants were drawn from a higher social class than the Regulars and were quicker to adapt to the rapidly changing conditions of warfare.

Backs to the sea. Black-uniformed Belgian Civil Guards in Antwerp.

CHAPTER III

THE BATTLE FOR BELGIUM

BY the end of August, the dimensions of the German drive through Belgium had become clear. Under considerable pressure, the Belgian Army had eluded destruction and fallen back on the fortress-port of Antwerp. At first with great reluctance, and then with increasing concern, Joffre began bolstering his left wing. Meanwhile, the British Expeditionary Force had landed, a small but powerful reinforcement. As the fighting along the Franco-German frontier subsided, a series of new battles erupted along the Franco-Belgian border.

By 20 August the French Fifth Army had concentrated inside Belgium, in the salient formed by the junction of the Meuse and Sambre rivers, with the mission of securing the French left, linking up with the Belgians, and preparing to strike at the German flank as they moved into Belgium. The Fifth Army commander, Charles Lanrezac, had been an early critic of Plan 17. Though his views were correct, he was an indecisive field commander. For 48 hours, Lanrezac was unable to decide whether or not to bring his army across the rivers or occupy the heights on their southern banks of the rivers or the high ground still further south. Instead, he deployed to the south of the rivers and awaited developments. Meanwhile, he looked to the west, where the British were expected to arrive.

The B.E.F.

Great Britain declared war on Germany on 15 August. Field Marshal Lord Kitchener was named to the Cabinet position of Secretary of State for War, a controversial appointment, for a military officer had never held this post before. At 64, Kitchener was still quite vigorous, heaving served nation and Empire for decades. Possessed of enormous prestige, he had swept away the followers of the Mahdi and ended a very difficult war against the Boers.

When the Cabinet authorized the dispatch of the B.E.F. to the Continent, Kitchener insisted that the assembly area be moved back from Maubeuge to Amiens. He was uneasy about the pace of the German advance, and worried that the B.E.F. might be attacked while still assembling in its marshaling areas. Kitchener shocked the Prime Minister and the Cabinet when he asked that the country be put on a war footing, for he believed the struggle would last more than three years. The new Secretary of State for War and the Prime Minister soon reached agreement that the army of 500,000 which Kitchener believed would be needed to fight the war would be raised from volunteers; no coercion would be used.

With the declaration of war, Sir John French was appointed to command the B.E.F. He had his work cut out for him. Kitchener spoke to him in a dual role, as Britain's senior serving Field Marshal and as a Cabinet member. Kitchener's view that that, in relation to the two major armies, those of France and Germany, the B.E.F. was too small to exercise a decisive role in the opening battles. As a result, he did not want the B.E.F. either decimated or destroyed.

French was informed that the primary objective of the B.E.F. was to cooperate with the French Army in preventing an invasion of Belgium or in repelling one. The neutrality of Bel-

85

Truly "the few," Belgian airmen in 1914.

Kitchener

Winston Churchill at the outbreak of war, as First Lord of the Admiralty. This was a governmental title and did not indicate that the holder was a member of the nobility.

Despite its antiquated appearance, the Belgian army fielded some experimental automobile units, which harassed the Germans to good effect.

British Maxim machine gun section on the march.

gium was to be restored. In the days ahead, the effort to fulfill these tasks would face enormous difficulties. The enemy was to prove remarkably strong and able and the allies stubborn and intractable. But inter-allied cooperation is always a very difficult matter, for differences in strategic plans, political aims, and simple routine are not easily understood or resolved.

On 12 August the main body of the B.E.F. began crossing the English Channel. Over the next five days an average of thirteen ships sailed daily from Southhampton to La Havre. Upon landing, the troops proceeded inland by rail, through Rouen to Boulogne. Sir John and his staff left Dover for Paris on 14 August. In Paris he met with the British Ambassador, Sir Francis Bertie, as well as with President Raymond Poincarie and Prime Minister Rene Vivani. The French were anxious to know when the B.E.F. would enter the battle. Sir John told them it would require ten days to assemble the army; nothing would happen before 24 August.

French children greet men of the Cameronians.

Passing French Dragoon

The first units to reach France were four divisions of infantry and one of cavalry. Kitchener kept back some regulars in Britain until arrangements could be made to defend against possible German landings. The corps and divisional commanders of the B.E.F. enjoyed good reputations inside the army. The Cavalry Division was commanded by Maj.-Gen. E.H.H. Allenby, who would later command a corps and then the army that defeated the Turks in Palestine. I Corps, under Lt.-Gen. Sir Douglas Haig, later commander of the B.E.F., consisted of the 1st and 2nd Divisions. The II Corps—the 3rd and 5th Divisions—was supposed to be led by Lt.-Gen. Sir J.M. Grierson, the ablest tactician in the British Army, but he died of heart failure on 17 August. Kitchener appointed Lt.-Gen. Sir Horace Smith-Dorrien in his place. Smith-Dorrien took command at Bavai on 21 August. This appointment was to have fateful consequences. Smith-Dorrien was generally liked by his contemporaries, but not by Sir John French. Their relations, at first cordial, would steadily deteriorate.

General Allenby in his pre-war dress uniform as Colonel of the 5th Royal Irish Lancers. Frustrated by lack of mobility on the Western Front, his true worth was displayed in Palestine in 1917.

"The man who disobeyed." Crusty Zulu War veteran Sir Horace Smith-Dorrien.

The spirit of the Royal Navy personified. The Chief of the War Staff, Vice-Admiral Sir Frederick Sturdee. Royal Naval actions in the North Atlantic in 1914, while little known, bottled up the German fleet for another two years. Sturdee commanded British forces in the Falklands in December.

While his army was assembling, Sir John French went to the headquarters of the French Fifth Army, for the B.E.F. would operate on its left flank. Lanrezac was not particularly impressed with Sir John. The latter's natural inability soon became apparent. His conduct was abrasive and outrightly rude. Neither of the two commanders spoke each other's language, so every conversation was channeled through interpreters. As time passed the French general became more agitated. After having had the general scope and direction of the German advance in Belgium explained to him, Sir John asked if Lanrezac thought the Germans planned to cross the Meuse. Lanrezac angrily replied, "Tell the Marshal that in my opinion the Germans have merely gone to the Meuse to fish!" While French's attitude was thick headed, Lanrezac's was outrightly insulting, but Brig.-Gen. Henry Wilson, French's sub-chief of staff, a confirmed Francophile, made a diplomatic translation to the Field Marshal. While both armies were in theory required to cooperate, both commanders left the meeting with the idea of having as little to do with each other as possible.

On 21 August the B.E.F. started to move forward to the line of Mauberge-Landrecies-Bohain, intending to assemble in the vicinity of Mons. Sir John French established his headquarters at Le Cateau.

Sir Henry Wilson in a general's uniform similar to the one in which he was assassinated in 1922.

THE 1914 CAMPAIGN

1

2

3

4

5

1) In a post-assassination black-bordered postcard of Crown Prince Franz Ferdinand, Order of the Golden Fleece is clearly visible at his throat. (2) Helmet and (3) blood-stained jacket are on exhibit with portrait and (4) car in which he and his wife were killed at the Vienna Museum of Military History. (5) Rare color postcard of period shows unusual night funeral procession of Franz Ferdinand and wife Sophia.

Leichenzug des Erzherzogs Franz Ferdinand und der Herzogin Sophie von Hohenberg.

Raemaeker's early political cartoon illustrates German attitude toward the "defenseless."

The creative sector of Imperial Germany reacted quickly to the martial atmosphere with posters. Munich artist Ludwig Hohlwein, creator of this poster, was already well known in the pre-war era.

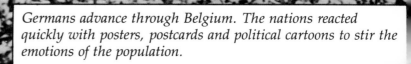

Germans advance through Belgium. The nations reacted quickly with posters, postcards and political cartoons to stir the emotions of the population.

This poster of Lord Kitchener served as the model for the famous "I want you!" Uncle Sam poster.

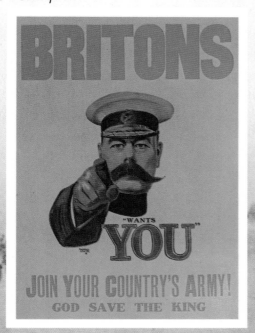

Women of Britain were encouraged to put enormous pressure on men to join the war effort.

THE HEROIC CHARGE OF THE ENGLISH CAVALRY AT THE BATTLE OF MONS
Jules Rouffet
Musée de L'Armée, Les Invalides, Paris

This painting by W.B. Wollen shows Canadians holding off a German charge. This scene prevailed during the next two years of the war: trench warfare, machine guns, grenades, mud and carnage.

Gen. Alexander von Kluck wears the Order of the Red Eagle.

Gen. Josef Jacques Césaire Joffre wears the Médaille Militaire.

Gen. Joseph Galliéni, Military Governor of Paris, wears the Star of the Legion of Honor.

Charleroi

While the B.E.F. was assembling, the German right wing had been sweeping through Eastern and Central Belgium. On 21 August *Generaloberst* Alexander von Kluck's *First Army* continued its advance to the southeast. While *Generaloberst* Karl von Bulow ordered his *Second Army* to continue its advance to the Sambre, *Generaloberst* Max von Hausen's *Third Army* closed up to a line a few miles east of the Meuse. Since the *Third Army* was not in its proper position, Bulow and Hausen agreed that their combined attack against Lanrezac's Fifth Army south and west of Namur would be postponed until the 23rd. On 21 August Lanrezac had finally ordered that the heights on the southern bank of the Meuse be occupied. As the French units approached these positions, they were attacked by advance units of Bulow's *Second Army*. After some little fighting, Bulow held his positions to await the arrival of Hausen's *Third Army*, which would be coming up on his—Lanrezac's—southern flank.

On the evening of the 21st, the right flank of the French Fifth Army took up defensive positions running from Fosse to Marchienne-au-Pont, while its left flank approached Thuin. With a cavalry screen covering his far left, Lanrezac decided to commit his reserves. One reserve division was on its way to relieve II Corps, which was guarding the army right, on the Meuse south of Namur. The other two reserve divisions moved north to Avegnes. Lanrezac waited to be attacked.

Close-up of guns on board H.M.S. Dreadnought.

Meanwhile, the right wing of the *Second Army* reached the line of the Canal du Centrè just north of Charleroi. Here its lead elements encountered French cavalry. The French were driven back. Bulow's left began operations against the eastern forts of the Namur complex, while his center came into contact with the French Fifth Army on the line of the Sambre and forced a river crossing. By the evening of 21 August the German *Second Army* had secured crossings of both the Canal du Centre and the Sambre.

On 22 August von Bulow tried to concentrate the units of the *Second Army* on the north bank of the Sambre and prepare for an advance across that river by the 23rd, to force a passage of the Meuse for the *Third Army*. The *First Army* was ordered to come into position to support the right of the *Second Army*. Bulow was given information that the French forces south of the Sambre were mostly cavalry and that their main forces were located along a line from Beaumont to Philippeville. Bulow was faced with a problem: should he continue to cooperate with the *First* and *Third Armies* or should he give up passage of the Sambre at little cost. He chose the first course. Bulow attacked at noon, on 23 August, having asked the *Third Army* to push forward.

Meanwhile Hausen's *Third Army* had received orders to move to the east bank of the Meuse and cross over. It was at this point that Bulow's messages arrived at Hausen's headquarters informing him that, contrary to previous orders and arrangements, the *Second Army* had crossed the Sambre, and asking for cooperation in the form of an advance across the Meuse.

The first Sea Lord, Prince Louis of Battenberg, soon to be Mountbatten. European members of the Royal Family resident in Great Britain with Germanic titles and surnames exchanged them for English equivalents, which they have borne to the present day.

Hausen hastened to cooperate, though some confusion resulted. Bulow's center had attacked the French in the direction of Metter and forced their line back. On his extreme left, infantry divisions came into line to relieve the cavalry, deploying along the south bank of the Sambre between Merbes Le Chateau and Manbenge.

Despite the lack of enemy resistance, Bulow's headquarters was not very optimistic. Kluck's *First Army* had failed to cooperate with Bulow's movements, while the *Third Army* had made little headway. Bulow was worried about the prospects for a French counterattack. The German troops were starting to show the effects of fatigue and there was a shortage of supplies. Nevertheless, a new attack was ordered for the 24th.

von Bülow

Dinant on the Meuse, the fortress above and the city below. The virtual impossibility of engaging such military targets without damage to civilians is obvious here.

On the morning of 24 August Lanrezac had orders issued for a general retreat to the line of Givet-Philippeville-Merbes-Le Chateau. Surprisingly, the Germans let the Fifth Army withdraw. The German *Second Army* advanced a few miles southward, the *Third Army* resumed its advance on Fumay, but did not cross the Meuse in force until 28 August. This was a bit of luck for Lanrezac. But he had promised to give Sir John French word if he was going to withdraw and he had failed to do so. The French Fifth Army thus exposed the B.E.F. on its left flank, while losing contact with the Fourth Army, to its right. The Germans poured through the gap between the Fourth and Fifth Armies and advanced unsuspectingly on the B.E.F. The nature of the campaign was changing.

On 24 August French intelligence informed Joffre that the rumors of the Germans using reserve formations in their battle line were actually true. Joffre started to make arrangements to

alter French dispositions so that he could deal with the German advances into Belgium and Northern France. Drawing troops from his right, Joffre tried to ease the crisis on his left by ordering the IX Corps—the Morroccan and 17th Divisions—to reestablish communications between the Fourth and Fifth Armies. It was a matter of "too little, too late." At 0300 on 28 August, even as the 17th Division attacked towards La Martee, the outposts of the Morroccan Division were themselves attacked by the *XII Saxon Corps.* By 1100 the Germans had forced the Morroccan Division back and took Signy L'Abbaye, opening the way to Rethel. Fortunately for the French, the Germans did not follow up their initial success. The situation stabilized over the next few days. Meanwhile heavy fighting broke out further to the west, as the B.E.F. went into action for the first time.

Pontoon bridge built by Germans to replace bridge in background destroyed by retreating British during the Marne campaign.

The *Third Army* began its attack into the French right early on the 24th. The French, in strong positions well adapted for defense, fought with determination. However by noon the German left had effected a crossing of the Meuse and the French started to retire. The combined attack of *Second* and *Third Armies* forced Lanrezac's Fifth Army back. Orders came in from Moltke's headquarters in Luxembourg; the *Third Army* was to move on Fumay, to cut off the French retreat. Even as this transpired, the army's center was fighting a fierce action at Dinant and managed to cross the river late in the day. The left, which attacked towards Outrage, was counterattacked and driven back by the French I Corps, under Louis Franchet d'Esperey. The advance on Fumay stalled. Nevertheless, the *Third Army* was across the Meuse. Hausen ordered a pursuit for the next day. Meanwhile, from the *Second Army* came a request for an attack westwards against the flank of the French Fifth Army. Hausen agreed and directed his right flank to move on Mettet. The Fifth Army was threatened with envelopment.

Lanrezac saw his flanks and rear in peril. He had been advised of the defeat of the Third and Fourth Armies in the Ardennes and felt that if the Fifth Army were to be destroyed, France would lose the war. He did not want to be responsible for another Sedan. Reports had come into his headquarters stating that the B.E.F. had been engaged for the whole day against superior numbers. Lanrezac knew that his troops had suffered heavy casualties and were exhausted. He decided to fall back.

The Oxford Hussars. Volunteers organized by Winston Churchill, Valentine Fleming, and other prominent civilians, they were trained to high enough standards to ride with the Regular cavalry in 1914. In peacetime they wore the Mantua purple forage caps worn here.

*French "spahis." The British Scots Greys dyed their
horses to make them less conspicuous.*

Mons

The British Expeditionary Force had advanced into the line on 21 August. The Cavalry Division formed the vanguard of the B.E.F. as it advanced, followed by II Corps under Smith-Dorrien and I Corps under Haig. On 21 and 22 August aircraft and cavalry patrols reported that hostile cavalry had arrived around Nivelles and that a substantial part of the enemy's main force was between Enghien and Charleroi. The B.E.F. deployed for battle. Unlike Wellington's Army, which a bare century earlier had fought among the rolling hills and farm lands of the nearby Waterloo battlefield, the B.E.F. was going to fight along the canals, drainage ditches, and slag heaps of the mining center of Belgium, terrain offering much in the way of natural defenses.

The British occupied a front running along the line Binche-Mons-Conde Canal. I Corps was on the right flank as far as Villers St. Ghislain and II Corps on the left, behind the Mons Canal. The 15th Cavalry Brigade covered the open right flank of the I Corps, while the rest of the Cavalry Division formed a line in front of the Canal, to a position east of Conde, in the rear of the left flank. Despite Lanrezac's failure to keep him informed, Sir John French had learned of the withdrawal of the French Fifth Army on his right flank. Available information suggested that a strong German force of some three or four army corps was advancing on his position. Abandoning any idea of offensive action, he decided that the B.E.F. should stand

its ground and wait for the Germans to attack. When Lanrezac requested a British counterattack to relieve his situation, Sir John replied that the best he could do was to hold his position for 24 hours.

Meanwhile, Alexander von Kluck of the German *First Army* was ordered to cooperate with and give direct support to von Bulow's *Second Army*. Kluck was not pleased with this state of affairs, for his army was supposed to set the pace, but agreed to swing his army southwards to the line of Lessines-Soignies. His cavalry had made contact with British cavalry on 22 August and Kluck had concluded that the B.E.F. was coming up to support the left flank of the French Fifth Army on the Sambre. He and Bulow now disagreed, Kluck wanted to deploy and attack the British left (II Corps), while Bulow insisted that the *First Army* should continue to support his movement across the Sambre. Finally, on 23 August, Kluck received orders to advance across the Canal du Centre to a line north of Maubeuge, the northeast of Conde. An unanticipated result of this was that it would bring him into contact with II Corps of the B.E.F.

British horse artillerymen wash up in a French railyard.

British cyclists. These appear to be infantrymen, rather than the more common Signals section of the Royal Engineers.

Irish Guards on parade. Formed in 1901 to supplement the English and Scottish Guards units, the 1914 campaign was to be their baptism of fire.

At 0530 on 23 August Sir John French met with his corps commanders, informing them that the army was to take defensive positions. I Corps would be on the right, to the northeast, between the Sambre and the Haine, southeast of Mons. It would form right angles to the line of II Corps and the 19th Infantry Brigade, which would face north along the line of the Canal du Centre, from Mons to just east of Conde. The B.E.F. was to be supported on its left by the French 84th Territorial Division while the British Cavalry Division was to be posted on the left rear of II Corps. This front measured some 4.3 kilometers. The ground along the canal was a built up area and the heights of the Haine, to the southeast, afforded strong second line positions in the rear.

Around 0900, elements of the German *First Army* attacked along the Canal line occupied by II Corps. The action became intense

Sir Douglas Haig in the uniform of the 17th Lancers, which formed his personal escort throughout the war.

British troops rest in a French town. Some beleaguered soldiers reported being rescued by angels and ghostly longbowmen. Modern historians and psychologists say they were just suffering from shell-shock....

and by 1100 was general all along the front, as the 3rd and 5th Divisions were beset by five German divisions. The Germans attacked in such dense formations that one British soldier described them as looking "Like a crowd coming up for Cup Day." The German infantry suffered from the skillful British shooting. So dense and effective was British rifle fire that German officers reported encountering machine gun companies. By the early afternoon the right of Smith-Dorrien's II Corps was forced to evacuate Mons and the Canal bend to the north of the town. The British troops retired to their second position.

On the right, Haig's I Corps was not seriously engaged nor were either the 19th Brigade

or the French Territorials on the extreme left. Despite being outnumbered by the attackers, British losses were not severe. The morale of the B.E.F. was still intact. At 0100 on 24 August the chief-of-staff of the B.E.F., Gen. Sir Archibald Murray summoned the staff offices of the two corps to a meeting. He informed them that Sir John French wished to conduct a withdrawal to a line between Longueville and La Boiserette. The delivery of the operational orders for this maneuver was, however, delayed for there was no telephone communication between the corps and B.E.F. headquarters at Le Cateau. Haig received his instructions only at 0200 while Smith-Dorrien received his only at 0300.

The pre-dawn withdrawal was done in the face of opposition and a number of casualties were incurred. The I Corps and the right flank of the II Corps made their way back easily, but the center and the left of II Corps and the Cavalry Division were attacked at Framieries and Elouges. Daylight on 24 August found the B.E.F. standing somewhat battered but intact on a line at Bavai. Surprisingly, the German *First Army* made almost no attempt to pursue the British, believing that they would remain in position on the defensive. When Kluck realized his mistake it was too late to carry out an enveloping movement with his right wing. The retirement from Mons saved the B.E.F. from annihilation. It also meant that the Allies were now everywhere in retreat.

British Lancers in camp. Their lances, stripped of penions to confound snipers and artillery observers have been pressed into practical use.

THE CAVALRY DIVISIONS

	Belg	Br	Fr	Ger	Ru
Manpower	4.5	9.5	5.4	4.5	4.2
Sabers	3.6	6.4	4.5	3.5	3.6
Rgts: Number	6	12	6	6	4
Men	0.6	0.53	0.75	0.58	0.9
MGs: Number	6	24	12	0	4
Ratio	1.6	3.7	2.8	0	1.1
Arty: Pieces	12	36	8	12	12
Ratio	3.3	5.6	1.8	3.4	3.3
Inf: Bns	1	—	0.5	1	—
Men	0.6	—	0.32	1.3	—
MGs	1	—	0	6	—
Engr Coys	1	1	1	1	—
Sig Sects	1	2	2	1	1
Aircraft	—	—	2	—	—

This table examines the strengths and organization of the cavalry divisions of the Western Front powers, with Russia added for comparison. Switzerland and The Netherlands have been omitted as they had no divisional organization for their cavalry. In all armies cavalry divisions were composed largely of active, regular professional soldiers rather than regulars mixed with reservists. There was little to choose from among the cavalry divisions of the European armies, aside from the British. The latter, building upon their experiences in South Africa, had developed the most flexible and capable cavalry divisions, so that they were essentially mounted rifle divisions, though they were not properly employed as such in this campaign.

The role of cavalry was to advance in front of the armies and gather information about the enemy, to cover the rear in retreats, and to pursue should the enemy be broken. Serving as mounted riflemen, the cavalry would have been capable of executing deep penetrations and other strategic maneuvers. That the British cavalry was not so

Footnote: Cavalry Divisions

All the 1914 armies had sizeable cavalry contingents, and these proved to be of some use in the opening phases of the campaign, particularly in reconnaissance and screening operations. However, 1914 was the last year in which large scale cavalry formations were employed in Western Europe, due primarily to the effects of the machine gun. What follows is a summary of cavalry division accessions during the campaign:

Belgium: one from 2 August through the week of 4 October, when a second was raised.

Britain: one was in France from 16 August, a second by 4 October, a third by 11 October, a fourth by 8 November, and a fifth by 20 December. Thus, by the end of 1914, nearly a third of the 16 British divisions in France were cavalry. Moreover, two of the cavalry divisions, those arriving in November and December, were composed of Indian personnel, as were two of the infantry divisions, which arrived in September and October, so that 25% of the British divisions in France by the end of the year were Indian.

France: ten divisions were on hand at the start of the campaign. An additional one was provisionally raised in the week ending 30 August, but disbanded by 13 September. A week later another provisional cavalry division was activated, which was disbanded by 18 October.

Germany: there were eleven cavalry divisions at the onset of the war, and nine of these served on the Western Front. No additional

divisions were raised.
employed was due partially to their small numbers, only one division in the most fluid period of the campaign, and partially to unimaginative leadership. The attachment of infantry to cavalry divisions was designed to strengthen their ability to engage in sustained combat and hold ground. In the German cavalry divisions the attached infantrymen—*jaegers*—were truckborne, an early example of motorization. Since British cavalrymen were all trained and equipped as infantrymen, there was no necessity to attach additional infantry. Russian cavalry lacked this training, and also the infantry, making their

divisions relatively less capable. Note that all the powers had assigned machine guns to their cavalry divisions, but that Germany had retained these in the attached infantry battalion, thereby decreasing the firepower of the mounted troops.

Key: *Manpower*, the total number of troops in the division in thousands. *Sabers*, the total number of officers and men equipped to fight as cavalry, in thousands. *Regts*, the number of cavalry regiments in the division—usually grouped in brigades of two or three apiece—along with the number of men per regiment. *MGs*, the number of machine guns in the

division, exclusive of those attached to the infantry, with the ratio per thousand sabers, a figure largely theoretical in the case of the Russian divisions. *Arty* is the number of light artillery pieces attached to the division, with the ratio of pieces per thousand sabers. *Inf* is the number of infantry battalions attached, with strength in thousands and machine guns. *Eng Coys* is the number of companies of engineers attached and *Sig Sects* the number of signal troops. The *Aircraft* assigned to the French cavalry divisions existed largely on paper.

British cavalry in one of many pre-war exercises on Salisbury Plain.

GERMAN LINES OF COMMUNICATION IN 1914

The Right Wing

First Army: Aacher-Liege-Brussels, then Cambrai on 26 August and Chaulnes on 30 August.

Second Army: Aachen-Liege-Fourmiers, and Hirson on 30 August.

Third Army: Staven-Liege until 31 August, then on a narrow gauge line to Tenn Roli, 11 kms south of Rocroi.

Fourth Army: Luxembourg; the railhead reached Seden on 1 September and Vousren on 8 September.

Fifth Army: This army soon found itself in grave difficulties because of demolition of tunnels near Montmedy, which was reached on 30 August.

The German Army supply lines were 125 kilometers from their main railheads.

CHAPTER IV

THE ALLIED RETREAT

THE close of 24 August found the strategic situation very precarious for the Allied side. The speed and weight of the German assault had been too great to be stopped by the initial French, Belgian, and British countermeasures. Moreover, the German Army enjoyed a numerical superiority. In the increasingly critical B.E.F. and Fifth Army sectors, 28 German divisions faced but 17 Allied ones. The Allies had not coordinated their actions nor had they arranged a proper concentration in the face of the enemy. The French Fifth Army had been moved to the Sambre too late to assist the Belgians and too far from the British to enjoy proper support from, or render aid to, the B.E.F. The French defeat at Charleroi nullified the limited British success at Mons. Fortunately for the Allied cause the Germans did not move quickly enough to take advantage of their strategic positions.

The Allied left now began a retreat, as the full weight of the German right gained momentum as it ground through Belgium. The hand at the helm might not be Schlieffen's, but his ideas sparked the German drive. How successful it would be depended on how effectively the right wing could maintain contact with the enemy.

Le Cateau

On the evening of 24 August Sir John French ordered the retirement of the B.E.F. from the area of Bavai to a position centered on Le Cateau. In order to effect his escape from the German advance he had to divide his force into two parts, for B.E.F. could not easily traverse the forest of Mormal. The I Corps was to march east of the forest, while the II Corps and the

Cavalry Division were to march down its western side. The period of grace granted by Kluck's inactivity soon came to an end, as the German *First Army* followed II Corps around the western end of the forest.

By 1700 II Corps had reached Le Cateau, while I Corps went into quarters for the night at Landrecies. There the rear guard of the I Corps was suddenly attacked by German units. Although this resulted in much confusion, the Germans were soon dispersed. Nevertheless, Haig, the I Corps commander, became somewhat alarmed. He reported the clash to Sir John, inflating its severity. Then he directed I Corps to retreat to the French lines at St. Quentin.

On the left flank of the B.E.F., at Le Cateau, the II Corps and the Cavalry Division were joined by the 4th Division, recently arrived from Britain. Considerable fighting had taken place that morning. As a result of Haig's report, Sir John believed that the right flank of his army was in peril. In reality, it was the left flank that would be the object of a German attack.

By the evening of 24 August Kluck had realized that he had misjudged the direction in which the B.E.F. would be moving. This was his second error in two days, for he had already miscalculated, having presumed a British intention to stand on the defensive the day before. Now both the British corps had eluded him. As a result, when his scouts reported a large concentration around Le Cateau, he changed the direction of his advance and headed straight for it. This brought *First Army* up against II Corps.

Smith-Dorrien had his headquarters at

British troops in street fighting at Landrecies. War artists usually underestimated the distance between opposing forces in engagements.

Bentry. His corps occupied a front of nearly 21 kilometers, from Le Cateay to Egnes. Allenby of the Cavalry Division came to II Corps to speak to Smith-Dorrien. The latter asked if the Cavalry Division could cover the retreat of the rest of II Corps. Allenby stated that his force could not do so because of fatigue and that the prospect of trying to move over roads clogged with refugees and transport did not help the situation.

Smith-Dorrien's units were still deployed along their broad front when he received orders to retire to the area of Busigny-Beaurevoir-Le Catelt. He decided to stand his ground rather than attempt a withdrawal in the face of the enemy and be overwhelmed piecemeal. If he could stop the advance of von Kluck's army he would be able to extricate himself. He would make a stand on the heights of the Le Cateau-Cambrai high road, between Le Cateau and Egnes. Meanwhile, the Germans came up. The German *First Army* halted for the night of the 25th-26th on the eastern edges of the Morma Forest. Kluck hoped that an attack in the morning would cut off the British retreat between Cambrai and St. Quentin.

At 0600 on the morning of 26 August elements of the British 4th Division were attacked by German cavalry and roughly handled before they could deploy on their assigned line at Liguy-Egnes. Once in position, however, the 4th Division stopped the German cavalry. On the opposite flank, the 5th Division, in and west of Le Cateau, was attacked and forced back to the heights southwest and west of the town. The Germans attempted to turn the right flank of the division in the Selle Valley, but this effort was frustrated with the help of the Cavalry Division. With the assistance of corps reserves the British positions were maintained.

British artillery passing through a French village. Extra forage is visible on the near side of some horses.

Royal Artillery 60-pounder in action. Heavy casualties at Mons and le Cateau shaped British artillery tactics for the rest of the century.

lgian infantry provide cover fire for an attempt to sabotage rail lines.

Tractor-drawn French heavy artillery. Horse-drawn artillery, even for the heaviest guns, was far more common.

The 3rd Division, in the center of II Corps, had not been heavily attacked on the morning of 26 August. As the day progressed, however, it was hit by a German army corps moving west from Landrecies. This move threatened to envelop the British right. When additional German units arrived along the front held by the 4th Division, pressure on the B.E.F.'s front intensified. At 1340 Smith-Dorrien ordered a general retirement, the orders reaching the units by 1500 hours. In this withdrawal the 3rd and 4th Divisions made an easy escape, but 5th Division lost some prisoners and guns before extricating itself.

The German *II Corps* attempted to intervene in the British retirement by attacking their left flank, but allowed themselves to be drawn into an attack on French Territorial forces near Cambrai and they were then engaged by the French cavalry near Crevecoeur. Thus, the British II Corps got away to the south. After an all night march over clogged roads amidst great confusion, Smith-Dorrien brought II Corps into the area of Bohain and Le Catelet. He had lost 8,000 men and 38 guns, but his corps was still a viable fighting force.

The II Corps, with the 4th Division and the Cavalry Division attached, now moved to St. Quentin and Ham, behind the line of the Somme, and then behind the Oise, where they established contact with the I Corps. They had fought a series of rear guard actions with the right wing of Bulow's *Second Army* and retreated through Etreux and Guise. By 29 August the B.E.F. was reunited as a fighting force. Now it stood on a line on the south bank of the Oise, between La Feue and Noyon. Here it received replacements, reorganized, and refitted. On 31 August the III Corps was formed under Maj. Gen. W.P. Pulteney, comprising the 4th Division and the 19th Infantry Brigade, to which would in due course be added the 6th Division, when it landed on 8 September. These maneuvers extricated the B.E.F. from a potential disaster. On their flanks, the French were also desperately trying to retrieve something from the disaster.

Members of the Royal Army Medical Corps at le Havre.

The Prince of Wales in Royal Navy uniform at the outbreak of war. The future Edward VIII, his expression suggests an ability to foresee the future.

Joffre's Reorganization

The collapse of Plan 17 did not unnerve Joffre. During 24-25 August, he calmly began to formulate new plans. The offensive clearly had failed, he had to prevent the envelopment of his left flank and he needed time to consolidate his forces to deal with the German Right Wing. He ordered Left Wing armies—including the B.E.F.—to retreat. On 25 August Joffre created the Sixth Army, under Maunoury, comprising the VII Corps and two reserve groups, and sent it to occupy a line from Cantiny through Montdidier. He began to draw troops away from the armies facing Alsace-Lorraine and send them to the Sixth Army.

French Dragoons armed with lances pass a British artillery column. White stockings on horses have probably been dyed to lessen visibility.

On 28 August Joffre wanted to start a limited offensive by the I Corps of the B.E.F. and the Fifth Army. However, by this time Sir John French was so unsettled that he refused Haig permission to cooperate in the action. The offensive was cancelled. Things grew worse. As the French General Staff was making plans to reorganize and realign their armies in order to stop the Germans from turning their left flank and eventually seizing Paris, the British commander stunned them by planning to withdrawn the B.E.F. from the fighting.

The Field Marshal believed that his army was in such poor shape that it could not carry on. Sir John proposed that he take the B.E.F. south-west, below the Seine river. He went so far as to give preliminary orders to this effect to his corps commanders. Haig, Smith-Dorrien, and the French were dumbfounded. In issuing this order, French had not consulted the Secretary of State for War or the Prime Minister. The director General of Communication for the B.E.F., Maj. Gen. Robb, sent Kitchener a copy of Sir John's proposal to take the B.E.F. out of the line and proceed south past Paris.

Immediately upon receiving Robbs' letter Kitchener made an inquiry of Sir John's intentions. The Secretary of State for War thought that such a withdrawal would permit the Germans to drive a wedge between the B.E.F. and the French Army. Conceivably the French Armies could be split into two groups. On 31 August Kitchener sent a telegram to Sir John French expressing astonishment and concern over his actions. Then Kitchener met with the Cabinet. He told the Prime Minister that if Sir John withdrew the B.E.F. in such a manner the Allies would lose the war. The Prime Minister told Kitchener to go to France without delay. By telegraph, Kitchener and Sir John agreed to meet at the British Embassy in Paris.

Kitchener pulled no punches at the meeting, at which the British ambassador to France and French liaison officer Col. Huguet were present. Sir John French noticed that Kitchener was wearing the uniform of a Field Marshal of the British Army. In this hour of uncertainty, Kitchener appeared as the senior serving Field Marshal in the British Army, French's superior by virtue of military rank, not civil office. Kitchener curtly informed Sir John of his intention to visit the troops in the field. Kitchener soon disabused Sir John of any idea of leaving the line. As a result of the visit of the Secretary of State for War there was a noticeable improvement in Anglo-French relations. The next step towards improving relations soon followed when Joffre removed the quarrelsome Lanrezac, an old friend but a failure as a commander, and replaced him with one of his corps commanders, Franchet d'Esperay, who was soon nicknamed "Desperate Frenchy" by the British enlisted men.

British assembly area in France.

French cyclists.

French anti-aircraft machine guns. Aircraft were not armed at this point and were more feared for the artillery fire they could bring down.

French airplane undergoing repairs.

Joffre—who would sack more generals in a shorter time than anyone in history—also replaced the Third Army commander, Ruffey, putting Maurice Sarrail, a leftist social Republican, in his place. Meanwhile, Joffre continued to build up the Sixth Army under Maunoury, whose command included the Paris Garrison, and created the Ninth Army under General Ferdinand Foch, a distinguished academy theoretician and the successful commander of XX Corps. By such measures, Joffre hoped to effect a reorganization of his forces in anticipation of a counter offensive to halt, and then reverse, the seemingly inexorable German advance in the north.

German strength began to wane as their offensive continued into September. The Belgian Army was still at Antwerp, watched by the *III Reserve Corps*. Two army corps had to be dispatched to the eastern front as a Russian advance panicked General Headquarters. The German Army had 67 divisions by 1 September 1914, as against 75 on 1 August.

German infantry pass through Amiens, August 31, 1914.

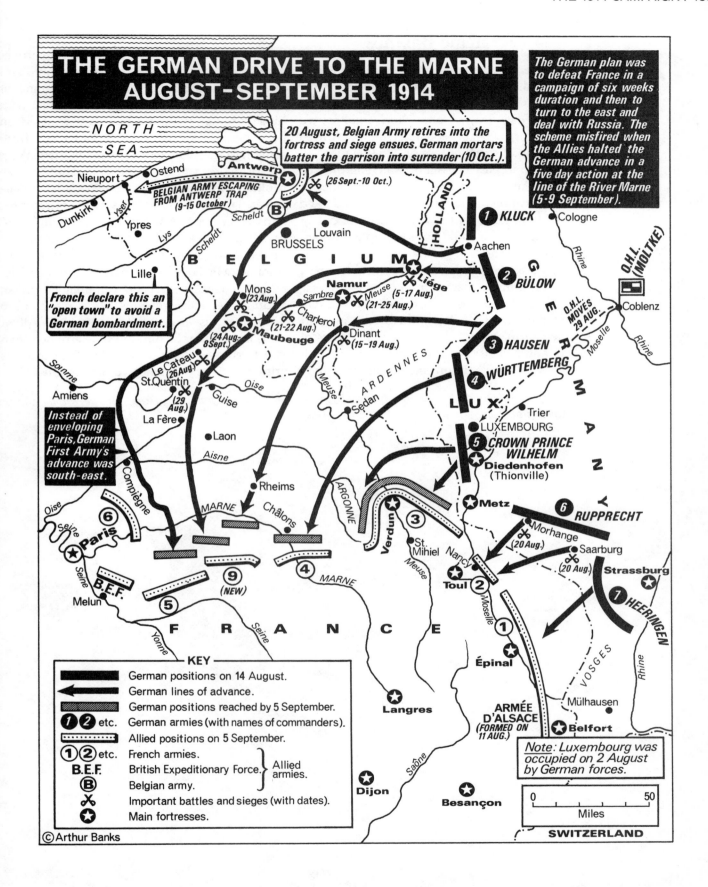

THE GERMAN DRIVE TO THE MARNE AUGUST–SEPTEMBER 1914

The German plan was to defeat France in a campaign of six weeks duration and then to turn to the east and deal with Russia. The scheme misfired when the Allies halted the German advance in a five day action at the line of the River Marne (5–9 September).

NORTH SEA

20 August, Belgian Army retires into the fortress and siege ensues. German mortars batter the garrison into surrender (10 Oct.).

BELGIAN ARMY ESCAPING FROM ANTWERP TRAP (9–15 October)

French declare this an "open town" to avoid a German bombardment.

Instead of enveloping Paris, German First Army's advance was south-east.

Nieuport
Ostend
Antwerp
Dunkirk
Ypres
Yser
Lys
Scheldt
Scheldt
(26 Sept.–10 Oct.)
HOLLAND
B
Louvain
BRUSSELS
Lille
BELGIUM
Mons (23 Aug.)
Sambre
Namur
Charleroi (21–22 Aug.)
Maubeuge (24 Aug.–8 Sept.)
Dinant (15–19 Aug.)
Meuse (21–25 Aug.)
Liége (5–17 Aug.)
Aachen
1 KLUCK
Cologne
2 BÜLOW
O.H.L. (MOLTKE)
Rhine
Coblenz
O.H.L. MOVES 29 AUG.
Moselle
Rhine
G E R M A N Y
3 HAUSEN
4 WÜRTTEMBERG
LUX
Trier
LUXEMBOURG
5 CROWN PRINCE WILHELM
Diedenhofen (Thionville)
6 RUPPRECHT
Morhange (20 Aug.)
Saarburg (20 Aug.)
Strassburg
7 HEERINGEN
Somme
Amiens
Le Cateau (26 Aug.)
St. Quentin (29 Aug.)
La Fère
Guise
Laon
Oise
Aisne
Sedan
ARDENNES
Meuse
ARGONNE
Verdun
St. Mihiel
3
Metz
Nancy
Toul
2
Moselle
Compiègne
Oise
Seine
6
Paris
B.E.F.
Melun
5
MARNE
Rheims
Châlons
9 (NEW)
4 MARNE
F R A N C E
Seine
Yonne
Seine
1
Épinal
VOSGES
Rhine
Mülhausen
ARMÉE D'ALSACE (FORMED ON 11 AUG.)
Belfort
Langres
Saône
Dijon
Besançon
SWITZERLAND

Note: Luxembourg was occupied on 2 August by German forces.

KEY

▬▬	German positions on 14 August.
◀▬	German lines of advance.
▨▨	German positions reached by 5 September.
❶❷ etc.	German armies (with names of commanders).
∙∙∙∙	Allied positions on 5 September.
①② etc.	French armies.
B.E.F.	British Expeditionary Force. } Allied armies.
Ⓑ	Belgian army.
✂	Important battles and sieges (with dates).
✪	Main fortresses.

0 ———— 50
Miles

© Arthur Banks

Strategic Balance

By early September the German Right Wing had been in almost constant action for thirty-two days. The three Right Wing Armies—the *First*, *Second*, and *Third*—had started with 17 corps. By 6 September they had been reduced to 12 corps, a loss of 225,000 men, all transferred to East Prussia or watching the Belgians at Antwerp or securing German lines of communications. The troops were tired, and short of supplies, as the logistical lines out of Aix-La-Chappelle could not keep up with operational demands.

By 6 September Joffre had created two new left wing armies, the Sixth and the Ninth. He had assembled a host which included the two new armies, the Fifth Army, the B.E.F., and part of the Fourth Army, which gave him a force of 41 Infantry divisions and eight cavalry divisions, with other reinforcements still coming in

from Lorraine. The German Right Wing armies could only field about 23 infantry divisions and five cavalry divisions. Since the beginning of hostilities Joffre had been in daily contact with his subordinates. Using a big touring car driven by a *Grand Prix* winner, he had raced from army headquarters to army headquarters along the primitive roads of the era. Thus, unlike Moltke, who remained at his general headquarters in Luxembourg, Joffre saw everything for himself. When he saw something he didn't like, he acted. By early September he had already sacked two army commanders, seven corps commanders, 20 infantry division commanders, and four cavalry division commanders in an effort to get abler generals. As a result, by 6 September his armies were better led. All of these changes made him more determined than ever to go over to the attack. The situation was grim but victory was not yet impossible.

A lumbering, utilitarian Henry Farman closes in on a fragile, graceful German Taube. In 1914 a whole world was coming to an end, both in the air and on the ground.

Germans dig a temporary trench. Extensive, connected trench systems were still a year away.

French 28cm howitzer. It was a fortress weapon not intended for the field use it is getting here.

INFANTRY WEAPONS, 1914

The technological improvements of the forty years prior to 1914 caused a number of problems for the armies of Europe. The situation with regard to infantry was very similar to that for the artillery. Weapons were stronger and more lethal. The use of black powder as a propellant for infantry rifles was discontinued by France in 1886, by Germany in 1888, and by Britain in 1894. The new propellants, cordite and nitrocellulose, produced little smoke and adoption of smokeless powder proved to be revolutionary. The soldier could fire from a great distance and not reveal his position. The dense clouds of smoke caused by black powder were gone. Moreover, rifles using smokeless powder did not foul and jam as easily as those using black powder. Accuracy and hitting power improved and the caliber of the rifles were reduced. Thus, France went from the 11mm Gras Rifle to the 8mm Lebel, German from the 11mm Mauser 71/84 to the 7.92mm Model 1888 Rifle, and later to the Model 1898. Soon almost every army in the world was shooting the new powder.

Tactically, a number of problems arose. Infantry now drew up in either skirmish formation or some kind of extended order. The platoon and company commanders could no longer ride up and down the line directing fire from horseback. Soldiers were either kneeling or prone while firing. During the South African War the British found that anyone who sat on a horse directing fire was immediately killed. Battle was now opened at great distances and the enlisted men had to be taught to shoot more

accurately and to select their own targets. Many officers were still uncertain about how much authority to relinquish to N.C.O.s and enlisted men.

The French Army adopted an 8mm cartridge in 1886; this was further modified by the adoption of a conical steel jacketed bullet in 1893. The basic rifle used was the 1886/93 Lebel, with an eight round magazine. It was a rather unique weapon; the magazine was a tube under the barrel and the rounds were pushed into the breech by a powerful spring. When the tube magazine was empty it took at least 60 seconds to reload under ideal conditions. If the fighting was intense the soldier was forced to use single rounds. This posed some real problems for platoon and company commanders. Volley fire by platoons and companies was still the approved method of fire. Company and platoon leaders were expected to count cartridges and direct the fire of their men. The French infantry would be at a significant disadvantage when fighting an infantry force armed with a more modern weapon. When war broke out there were almost three million Lebel rifles in service and in storage for the reserves. The combat load of ammunition for a French infantryman was 120 rounds carried in three pouches on his belt.

The French army adopted their first modern machinegun in 1904. The Puteaux gun was an 8mm piece with a rate of fire of 450–500 rounds per minute. In 1907 the French adopted an improved machinegun, the St. Etienne, which was followed in 1914 by the Hotchkiss. French machineguns were

unusual in that they were air cooled, not water cooled, like German ones. This made them lighter and more easily transported. These weapons had an additional unusual feature, for they used a 24-round metal clip instead of a 250-round cloth belt. Each of the guns weighed between 50 and 60 pounds and at that were light when compared to their German and British counterparts. The tactical use of these weapons was conservative and essentially defensive, for the Grandmaison School did not have a high opinion of weaponry that did not lend itself to maneuver.

The German infantry was both well equipped and well trained. Their standard issue rifle, the 7.92mm Model 1898 Mauser was one of the best, with a five round stripper clip. This device permitted the cartridges to be slipped into a magazine and the metal clip to be discarded. The magazine could also be loaded by placing individual rounds through the top of the magazine. The previous piece, the 1888 Commission Rifle, used a five round Mannlicher-style magazine, in which the clip was an integral part of the magazine mechanism, and thus would not accept individual rounds except in the breech. By 1914 this rifle was relegated to reserve duty.

The Model 1898 Mauser was issued in three versions, the standard long rifle, a short rifle, and a cavalry carbine. The regular infantry used the long 1898 Mauser, while the Kar. 1898 short rifle was issued to jaeger battalions and engineer troops. The combat load of ammunition was 150 rounds per man. The troops were taught to shoot well, to select their own targets but fire on the command of their platoon and company commanders. Some officers felt that target shooting alone lacked sufficient realism when compared to actual combat.

The prewar army had used large numbers of machineguns in active operations in Africa and China and on maneuvers. The Germans experimented with a number of ways of transporting these guns. The standard machinegun was the 7.92mm Model 1908, which, when combat ready, weighed 137 pounds. It was cooled by means of a metal jacket over the gun barrel which had to be filled with water at regular intervals while the weapon was in action. The Germans chose to use the machinegun in both offensive and defensive operations. Defensively, they used it with devastating effects on the French infantry during the Battle of the Frontiers. They also used massed indirect fire to support their infantry in the attack and to harass the enemy infantry in its attempts to defend its positions. A number of German officers were conscious of the effects of modern weapons; however it took the shock of actual combat to convince many others.

The British were at least four years behind the French and Germans in the adoption of a rifle using smokeless cartridges. However, by 1914 they were one of the more advanced armies in the design and use of infantry weapons. Their experiences during the South African War were responsible for many changes in equipment and

German machine-gun unit in improvised trench. Note the small size of the helmet in proportion to the head, an affectation of many German soldiers, especially officers.

training. The standard service rifle was the Lee Enfield Mk. I and its improved version, the Lee Enfield Mk. II, which, except for changes in sighting, was virtually the same weapon. This was a reasonably accurate rifle, with a .303 round nosed lead bullet propelled by cordite. The rifle had a ten round magazine, which was not, however, clip loaded. If the soldier used up ten rounds he could load the weapon with single rounds or try to reload the magazine. This was not an unreasonable task when operating against an opponent that had few if any firearms. Unfortunately, the Boers were using modern clip loading Mauser rifles and they proved to be excellent shots. In the initial stages of the South African War they had slaughtered hundreds of British soldiers.

The British were appalled to discover that their infantry could not shoot as well as the Boers. The factors that contributed to this problem were obvious. Colonial policing had been the main task assigned to the army since the Napoleonic Wars. Save for the Crimean War, the British had not faced a modern army in nearly a century. Then too, there was the parsimony of the Exchequer, which permitted only 60 practice rounds a year. The service rifle proved to be accurate enough when at last the soldiers were given enough time and ammunition to learn proper

Russian machine-gunners with Maxims.

marksmanship. The conditions of warfare against the Boers were such that a force of mounted infantry had to be raised. They were given the infantry long rifle because the issue cavalry carbine proved to be absolutely useless; the Boers normally opened fire at ranges of 500 to 1,000 yards while the carbine barely had a range of 200–300 yards. This demonstrated the need for a new service rifle that could be used by all branches of the army, a universal rifle. In January 1907 the Short Magazine Lee Enfield Mark III rifle was approved. It was 3'8.5" in length and weighed 9.7 pounds. The new rifle, almost a foot shorter than its predecessor, used a magazine of ten rounds and could be loaded by using ten round stripper clips, which permitted rapid reloading even under fire. The infantry, the cavalry, the artillery, and the engineers all used the same weapon.

The musketry standards rapidly improved. Both officers and enlisted men were taught the fundamentals of good shooting. The British Army instituted extensive tactical training for platoons, companies, and battalions and in less than a decade was transformed into what was probably the best shooting force in Europe. The men learned how to pick targets at great distances and to fire on them effectively. Rapid fire exercises became common, for the Mark III could be fired accurately at up to 20 rounds a minute, an exercise called the Mad Minute, which was to shock the German infantry in Mons and elsewhere in Belgium. Despite these enormous changes, tradition lived on; the British Army Drill and Musketry Regulations did not drop forming square and volley fire until 1939.

In 1912 the British Army introduced a new machinegun, the Vickers Model 1912, which fired 450 to 550 rounds per minute, fed by 250 round cloth belts. When compared to its German counterpart, the Vickers was a wonder at only 88.5 pounds. Mounted on a tripod which permitted a traverse to the right and to the left and gave a good field of fire, watercooled Vickers machine remained in service into the 1960s.

The standard rifle used by the Belgian infantry was the Mauser 7.65mm Model 1889. It had a five round magazine which was loaded by using stripper clips. The Belgian cavalry and mounted gendarmerie used the Mauser Model 1889 carbine, which, except for its length, was identical to the rifle.

At the beginning of the war, the Belgian army possessed 102 machineguns. These were the French Model 1914 Hotchkiss, which weighed 52 pounds and fired 450–500 rounds per minute loaded by 24 round clips, and the Model 1909 Hotckhiss Light Machinegun, which weighed a remarkable 26 pounds and used a 30 round metal clip. Both weapons were 8mm. Thus the Belgians, who had one of the smallest and poorest armies in Europe, were the only combatants in 1914 to use a light machinegun until the arrival of the Indian Corps in September.

The standard heavy watercooled and aircooled machineguns needed extra care to stay in the field. The average heavy machinegun crew numbered between four and six men, for the weapon required a gunner, an assistant gunner, and at least two ammunition bearers, while one man of the crew had to be trained as an armorer to deal with the various

British infantry section with Maxim machine gun.

types of malfunctions that still plagued these weapons. Despite their operational problems, these weapons took advantage of the changes in metallurgy and propelants during the previous forty years. None of the rapid fire weapons of the 1870s or the 1880s could come close to their performance. Their value to a battalion or to a company was enormous, especially in defensive situations, even if they were clumsy. The light machinegun had none of these disadvantages, and most of the advantages.

The Belgians, the first to use them, issued their light machinegun to the carabiniers. Older machineguns, such as the watercooled Maximum heavy machine gun, were still issued to a number of units. The Belgian Army was also innovative in its methods of transportation, using two wheeled dog carts to move machineguns and ammunition at a time when the conventional methods were to use converted artillery carriages, pack horses, or sleds.

Despite its modernity in many areas, sartorially, the Belgian Army of 1914 appeared out of place in a modern war, looking almost as if it had just stepped out of a painting of the Battle of Waterloo. The regular infantry wore a black leather shako, a dark blue French style overcoat, and green trousers, while the carabiniers wore a Tyrolian style leather top hat, the Cyclist Carabiniers, brimless pill box hats, and their cavalry splendid green and red uniforms.

Canadian Highlanders in London. All British and Commonwealth Highlanders wore khaki aprons over the kilt. Rifles appear to be obsolete Lee-Metfords which will be replaced by Lee-Enfields before going to France.

Canadian mobile machine-gunners. These appear to be F.W.D. model B 3-ton lorries with improvised armor plating.

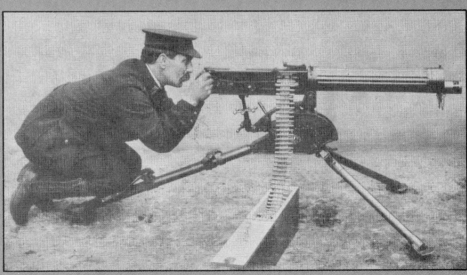

British Vickers machine gun. It was still being used at Suez in 1956.

INFANTRY WEAPONS OF THE 1914 CAMPAIGN

Piece		Cal	Wt	Ln	Rng	RPM	Mag	Note
Rifles								
Belg	Mauser F.N. 1889	7.65	4.0	1.3	2.0	10–15	5	A
Brit	Lee-Enfield No 1	7.7	3.3	1.1	2.0	15–20	10	B
Fr	Lebel M 1886/93	8.0	4.2	1.3	2.0	8–10	8	C
	Berthier Fusil 1907	8.0	3.8	1.3	2.0	10–15	3	D
Ger	Mauser M 1898	7.92	4.2	1.2	2.0	10–15	5	E
	Mauser M 1888	7.92	3.8	1.2	2.0	10–15	5	F
Machine Guns								
Belg	Hotchkiss M 1914	8.0	52.6	1.3	2.0	450–500	24–30	G
Brit	Vickers M 1912	7.7	40.9	1.1	1.0	450–550	200	H
Fr	Hotchkiss M 1914	8.0	52.6	1.3	2.0	450–500	24–30	G
Ger	MG M 1914	7.92	63.7	1.1	2.0	450–500	200	I

Notes: *Piece* is the designation of the weapon; *Cal*, caliber in millimeters; *Wt*, weight in kilograms, without bayonet in the case of rifles, which could add up to .5 kg; *Ln*, length in meters, without bayonet, which could add an additional .5 m; *Rng*, maximum range in kilometers, but most armies set sights to c. 400 meters; *RPM*, for rifles this is the number of aimed shots per minute possible at 400 meters presuming a well-trained man, for machine guns this is cyclic rate, the theoretical maximum number of rounds per minute, with normal rate being about half that given; *Mag*, is the number of rounds in the magazine; *Note*, refers to details given below.

A. Five round external box magazine.

B. Ten round box magazine ("clip").

C. Eight round tabular magazine.

D. Three round box magazine.

E. Five round integral box magazine.

F. Five round clip.

G. Ammunition came in round metal canister. Weight given includes tripod (27.7 kg) and water (c. 3.5 kg).

H. Ammunition came in canvas belts. Weight includes tripod (22.7 kg) and water (c. 3.5 kg).

I. Ammunition supply by belts. Weight includes tripod (34.1 kg) and water (c. 3.6 kg).

CHAPTER V

THE MARNE

As the German *First Army* moved southeast a large gap had developed between it and the *Second* and *Third Armies*. The gap was held by *Generalleutnant* Georg von der Marwitz's *II Cavalry Corps*, of three small divisions. The German movement had been closely watched by Allied air and cavalry reconnaissance. The gap was soon detected. Joseph Gallieni, the able military governor of Paris, informed Joffre, and Maunoury, commander of the Sixth Army, about the gap. Sensing an opportunity, he proposed that the Sixth Army attack into the gap at once. Joffre demurred; he wanted an attack to begin a few days later, in order to gain time to bring additional troops in from Lorraine and to plug up gaps in the lines of his own right flank armies. There was a serious gap between Foch's Ninth Army and Langle's Fourth Army, and between Langle's Fourth Army and Sarril's Third Army. Sitting imperturbably beneath an old tree, Joffre considered Gallieni's proposal, with no expression on his pudgy face. Then he decided. He issued "General Instruction No. 6" authorizing an offensive for 6 September.

By midmorning on 6 September the armies were deployed for the attack. The Sixth Army would strike Kluck's flank and push the Germans over the Ourcq River, while the B.E.F. was to attack into the gap in the direction of Montmirail. Further to the east, the Fifth Army was to attack due north, while Foch's Ninth Army was to hold the weight of the German Center; prepared to meet any attack from Bulow's *Second Army* and Hausen's *Third Army*, it had to cover the offensive of the Fifth Army.

The Germans had been hoping to preclude any French offensive by disrupting their eastern lines. Their *Sixth Army* made a determined attempt to take Nancy, but was soundly defeated by Castelnau's Second Army. The French were showing a remarkable resilience and it was beginning to trouble Moltke.

Moltke sent Staff Colonel Hentsch to examine the tactical and strategic condition of the *First*, *Second*, and *Third Armies*. Acting on Moltke's behalf, the Colonel spoke with his authority. Thus, peculiarly, a colonel could order the army commanders to alter their operational plans. By 5 September Kluck learned that the attack on Nancy had failed. Like Moltke, he began to become uneasy. He realized that he was now in danger of being enveloped by the French Sixth Army and the B.E.F. and cut off. The stage was set for one of the most critical actions of the century.

The Battle of the Marne began on the morning of 6 September. In its sector the B.E.F. advanced slowly, I Corps on the right, II Corps in the center, and III Corps on the left. The terrain towards the Marne was difficult, giving cover to rear guards and cut by two unfordable rivers, the Grand and the Petit Morin. Nevertheless, the II and III Corps encountered no opposition as they advanced, but I Corps ran into von der Marwitz's cavalry east of Rozoy and was pushed back. Wary of attempting to move through the forests of Crecy and Malvoisine, which lay on his left, Haig halted and waited for support in the form of II Corps. With a large British force at hand the Germans withdrew. Haig resumed his advance.

The progress of the French Armies was also slow. Their cavalry moved out and spent the day skirmishing with the enemy's rear guards, mostly infantry of the German *II Cavalry Corps*, consisting of a few jaeger and cyclist

Early German trench at the Marne, showing zig-zag pattern.

Royal Artillery howitzer being brought up to the Marne.

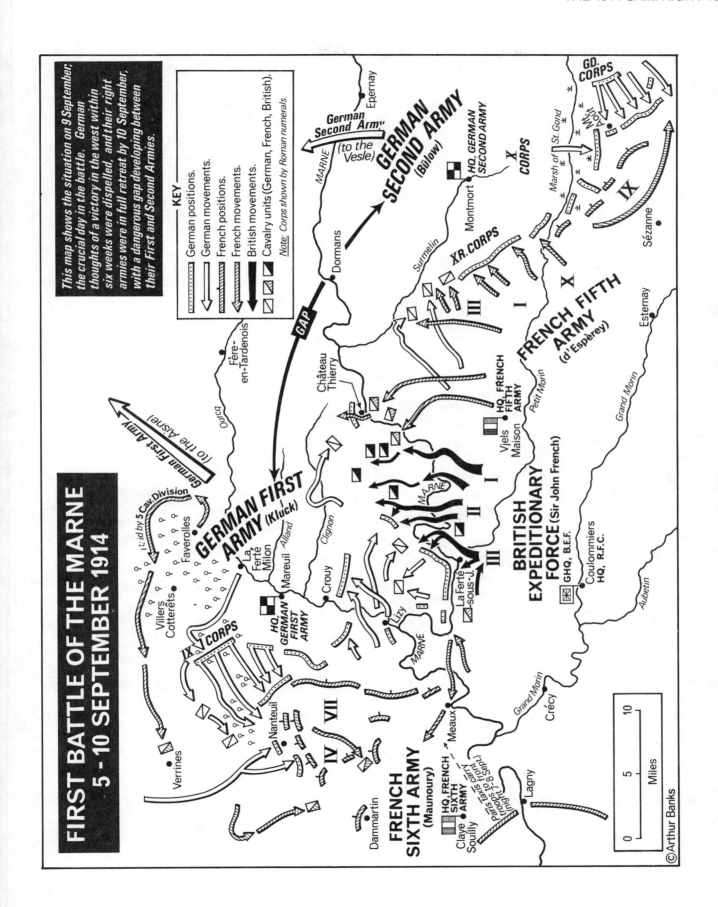

FIRST BATTLE OF THE MARNE
5 – 10 SEPTEMBER 1914

This map shows the situation on 9 September, the crucial day in the battle. German thoughts of a victory in the west within six weeks were dispelled, and their right armies were in full retreat by 10 September, with a dangerous gap developing between their First and Second Armies.

KEY

- German positions.
- German movements.
- French positions.
- French movements.
- British movements.
- Cavalry units (German, French, British).

Note: Corps shown by Roman numerals.

German Second Army (to the Vesle)

GERMAN SECOND ARMY (Bülow)

Epernay

MARNE

Dormans

GAP

Fère-en-Tardenois

Ourcq

German First Army (to the Aisne)

GERMAN FIRST ARMY (Kluck)

HQ, GERMAN SECOND ARMY

Montmort

XR. CORPS

X CORPS

GD. CORPS

Marsh of St. Gond

Mot

IX

Sézanne

Surmelin

III

I

X

FRENCH FIFTH ARMY (d'Espèrey)

Esternay

Grand Morin

Petit Morin

Château Thierry

HQ, FRENCH FIFTH ARMY

Vjels Maison

MARNE

I

II

III

La Ferté-sous-J.

BRITISH EXPEDITIONARY FORCE (Sir John French)

GHQ, B.E.F.

Coulommiers
HQ, R.F.C.

Aubetin

Crécy

Grand Morin

Lagny

id by 5 Cav. Division

Faverolles

La Ferté Milon

Mareuil

Ailand

Crouy

Clignon

Lizy

MARNE

Villers Cotterêts

HQ, GERMAN FIRST ARMY

IX CORPS

Nanteuil

IV VII

Verrines

Dammartin

Meaux

FRENCH SIXTH ARMY (Maunoury)

HQ, FRENCH SIXTH ARMY

Claye Souilly

Paris taxis carried troops to front (night 7-8 Sept.)

Scale

0   5   10

Miles

© Arthur Banks

German prisoners on the road to Paris. Some French Cuirassiers wore khaki helmet and breast-plate covers.

Sir Douglas Haig as lieutenant general.

Foch

batallions, well supplied with machineguns; German cavalry were armed with carbines and had no bayonets, nor were they trained in infantry tactics. That night the British halted with their left well beyond the Grand Morin while their right still lay behind the river.

By 7 September the British movement had brought them even with the French Fifth Army, a penetration of about a dozen kilometers. On the left Maunoury's Sixth Army found itself pressed. Manoury's troops had opened the ball on 6 September by attacking the German *IV Reserve Corps*, covering Kluck's exposed right along the Ourcq River. When this began to give way, Kluck had shifted the bulk of his *First Army* to its support, thus widening the gap between himself and the *Second Army*. This move proved an error on his part, for it facilitated the advance of the B.E.F., while only slowing that of the Sixth Army. Late on 7 September Maunoury's troops reached the Petit Morin.

In the center, Allenby's cavalry screened the movement of the B.E.F.'s I and II Corps, as they attempted to cross the river at several points in the face of determined German resistance. The III Corps advanced on La-Fente-Sous-Jouarre, located at the junction of the Petit Morin and the Marne. The Germans stoutly defended the town. The lead elements of the 4th Division were held in check, and had to wait for their artillery to be brought forward.

Meanwhile, Haig's I Corps captured the bridge at the town of Becherelle when a battalion of the Worcestershire Regiment stormed it backed by two battalions of the Guards. The Germans retired from the northern bank. Meanwhile, the 3rd and 5th Divisions, in the center, saw stiff fighting, but managed to force a passage across the river, and advance to within 1500 meters of the Marne. At Le Fente the German fire stopped an hour after the artillery of the 4th Division opened up and by nightfall the division held that part of the town which lay south of the Marne.

A battery of Royal Horse Artillery 18-pounders.

German horse artillery stays close to the trees while coming down a French road.

Cuirassiers leave Paris for the front.

The French armies on the right were heavily engaged and had made little progress on both 7 and 8 September. The Ninth Army, under Foch, was just able to hold off the combined weight of two German armies, the *Second* and *Third*. Franchet d'Esperey's Fifth Army managed to advance very slowly: while his center faced Bulow's *Second Army*, his left had a completely open path. Maunoury's Sixth Army, on the Ourcq to the left of the B.E.F., was struggling fiercely to advance but was finally pushed back by the weight of Kluck's *First Army*. The need to reinforce the Sixth Army was so great that two regiments of infantry, some 6,000 troops from the Paris Garrison, were brought up to the front, a distance of 60 kilometers by 600 taxis and buses, the former with their meters patriotically ticking away the whole time. It was the first use of motorized infantry in combat and brought hope that Maunoury could at least hold his ground.

British Dennis 3-tonner, in use here as a traveling repair shop.

French troops take an hour break. Blue-grey covers hide their red kepis, but the highly visible red trousers remain.

On the evening of 8 September Joffre issued "General Instruction No. 19." In it, he observed that the right wing of the German Army was divided into two groups, the only link between them was that provided by what remained of the *II Cavalry Corps*. He stated that an effort must be made to defeat Kluck before he could be reinforced by detachments from the units that had been released by the fall of hitherto besieged Maubege. The Sixth Army and the B.E.F. were given this task, the Sixth to tie the Germans down on the right bank of the Ourcq, while the B.E.F. crossed the Marne between Nogent l'Artand and La Fente-Sous-Jouarre. The British would move against the left flank and rear of Kluck's *First Army*, cutting him off. The Fifth Army was to cover the right flank of the B.E.F. by attempting to seize Chateau-Thierry.

On 9 September the B.E.F. continued its advance to the north, while a cavalry screen maintained contact with the French armies on either flank. The British thought that they would encounter stiff opposition. They were wrong. Resistance was light and many bridges were still intact. By 0900 the advanced guard of II Corps had penetrated over six kilometers into Kluck's left flank on the Ourcq. The progress of the II and I Corps was slower, as they were delayed by stouter enemy resistance, destroyed bridges, and a threat to the flank of I Corps emanating from Chateau-Thierry. This delay allowed the Germans to organize defensive positions along the line Chateau-Thierry-Lizy road and to hold on until nightfall.

Germans headed for the Marne try not to look at the column of ambulance wagons headed the other way.

Funeral procession for German artillery officer passes through French village. It's no place for a cameraman.

French medics with horse-drawn ambulance.

On 8 September Moltke again sent Col. Hentsch to tour the German armies. Hentsch saw the commanders of the *Fifth*, *Fourth*, and *Third Armies* and thought they were doing well. He found *Second Army* Headquarters a gloomy place, with Bulow on the verge of collapse, worrying about his exposed right flank. Hentsch concluded that *Second Army* would be forced to retreat. On 9 September he discussed the situation with Kluck's chief-of-staff. In view of the British advance to the Marne, they decided that the present line could not be held. At noon, using Moltke's authority, Hentsch ordered *First Army* to retreat to Soissons. The Battle of the Marne was over.

Quarries occupied by the Germans at Soissons.

German siege guns of the type that reduced Liege and Namur.

ARTILLERY

German 21cm howitzer.

Each of the armies had developed unique ideas concerning the employment of field guns and howitzers. The types of guns were determined by two factors, technical improvements in metallurgy and explosive propellants, and experience in active operations since the latter part of the nineteenth century. Technically, guns had become stronger and more powerful and steel had replaced bronze as the preferred metal for construction. Propellants such as picric acid and nitroglycerine replaced black powder. The new propellants left no thick clouds obscuring the battlefield and revealing their firing positions. With the increase in range, indirect fire became tactically more significant. As a result, new techniques for the laying and sighting of artillery pieces had to be developed.

In terms of their experience each army was unique, but the British and French had most of it, primarily in fast-moving colonial campaigns, while the Germans had very little.

The French Army had long placed its faith in the 75mm M97 field gun. However, the Supreme War Council gradually became concerned about the imbalance in the French artillery. By 1910 there

were no medium guns in service and the only heavy artillery was in coastal or frontier fortresses. While the members of the Supreme War Council expressed concern about the army's artillery, they reached no clear decision on how to deploy proposed heavier guns. The main issue was whether to assign medium guns to the army or corps level; no decision was made until the war broke out. A new 105mm field gun was authorized in 1913 but very few were produced before the war. Although the design for a 155mm howitzer had just been authorized, it would not see service until 1915. As a result, early in the war obsolete pieces of 120mm to 155mm were taken from forts and modernized by being put on field carriages. These pieces had to be towed by trucks because of their weight.

The Belgian Army largely imitated the French and shared French shortcomings in artillery.

Ther German Army was well supplied with all types of artillery. Germany put 642 batteries in the field in August of 1914, the guns ranging from the 77mm field piece to the gigantic 420mm siege howitzer. This combination gave the Germans a substantial advantage tactically in both the offense and the defense. The range and shell

weight would take a deadly toll of the French infantry. The German investment in artillery before the war would prove valuable in the initial operations in Belgium and France.

The British Army placed great faith in its 13- and 18-pounder field guns. The 13-pounder, specifically meant to be used as a cavalry support weapon, was assigned to the Royal Horse Artillery which served with the Cavalry Division of the B.E.F. The infantry divisions were supplied with the 18-pounder, the 4.5" howitzer, and the 60-pounder heavy field gun. The British preferred mobility and shell weight to range. They would eventually find that the 13-pounder was lacking in range and hitting power. The British and other armies would discover that modern artillery was becoming too heavy for horse-drawn transport. Indeed, guns larger than 6" were so heavy that they had to be moved by rail and towed by motor vehicles.

PRINCIPAL ARTILLERY PIECES OF THE CAMPAIGN OF 1914

This table sets forth the principal technical details of the bulk of the artillery pieces used on the Western Front in 1914, omitting only some miscellaneous pieces committed by all the armies. The significant differences in the artillery parks of the armies on the Western Front in 1914 were not technological, though there were some important technical differences. Thus, the French 77mm M1897 field gun could fire almost twice as fast as the equivalent Belgian, British, and German pieces. However, technology was not as important as doctrine. Thus, while French and the Belgians were equipped almost exclusively with light field guns, and the British had a modest allotment of heavier ones, over a third of the German artillery was composed of heavier pieces. In addition, the Germans had a small number of very heavy guns, includ-

Army	Piece	On Hand	Range (km)	Shell (kg)
Belg	75mm M05	?	9.9	6.5
Br	13-lb QF H.A.G.	245	5.4	5.7 [12.5 pds]
	18-lb QF Mk 1	1,126	6.0	8.4 [18.5 pds]
	60-lb BL Mk 1	28	9.4	27.3 [60.0 pds]
	4.5" Hwtzr	182	6.7	15.9
Fr	75mm M97 Fld Gun	2,800	6.9	7.3
	105mm M13 Fld Gun	50	12.7	15.3
	155mm Rimailho Hwtzr	?	5.5	45.0
	155mm L Hwtzr M77/14	?	13.6	45.0
Ger	77mm M96/06	5,000	8.4	6.8
	105mm Lt Hwtzr M98/09	1,650	7.0	12.7
	150mm Fld Hwtzr M02	600	8.5	40.0
	210mm Hvy Hwtzr M	84		
	305mm Skoda Hvy Mtr	12		
	420mm Hwtzr L/14	4	9.4	818.2

ing 84 210mm heavy howitzers, which were allocated to field army headquarters or held, together with a dozen Austrian Skoda 305mm heavy mortars and four 420mm Krupp siege mortars, by general headquarters for use against fortresses. While most of the artillery pieces indicated above were horse-drawn, the very heaviest pieces in the German inventory were pulled by tractors.

Key: *Piece* indicates the formal designation of the weapon in question, with its caliber [Abbreviations here are: *B.L.*, breach loading, a characteristic, in fact, of all pieces shown on this table; *Fld.*, field; *H.A.G.*, horse artillery gun; *Hwtzr.*, howitzer; *lb*, pounder; *Lt.*, light; *M*, model, usually with year of design given and sometimes with two, as "98/09" to indicate a modification of the original model; *Mk*, mark, the British way of saying model; *Mtr.*, mortar; *Q.F.*, quick firer, with automatic recoil mechanism, permitting sustained fire with minimal relaying]. *On Hand* indicates the number of pieces of this type committed to the Western Front in the period August-November of 1914, a figure which has in some cases been estimated, and where unknown has been indicated by a question mark. *Range*, the distance which the piece was normally expected to throw a shell, given in kilometers. *Shell*, the weight of the standard ammunition, given in kilograms [for British pieces the weight in pounds has also been indicated, to demonstrate that the older system of indicating caliber by poundage designations was rather inaccurate].

Footnote: Ammunition

Ruins of the Library at Louvain. Debate about German "atrocities" in Belgium continues to the present day, but neither side had any experience with modern weapons in populated areas.

In general, all of the pieces shown could fire high explosive shell. Pieces of 155mm and smaller caliber could also fire shrapnel, anti-personnel explosive shell. Heavier pieces, such as 210mm howitzers, were primarily anti-fortress and were served with armor-piercing or concrete-piercing shells.

None of the countries came close to properly estimating ammunition requirements. Their calculations ultimately were based on Franco-Prussian War experience, during which the Prussian field artillery had fired a daily average of 1.9 rounds per gun, a figure not seriously exceeded in any subsequent conflict. Since conventional wisdom dictated that the war was not going to last more than a year, it was simple enough to estimate that no more than 700 rounds was likely to be needed. Indeed, on the basis of experience and the presumed probable duration of a major war, the available stockpiles of artillery ammunition were rather generous.

At the outbreak of the war all of the armies had available about 1000 to 1500 rounds per gun. For the handful of very heavy guns, far smaller ammunition allotments were maintained, in the case of the 305mm and 420mm pieces only a few dozen rounds each. Since ammunition expenditure in the campaign often reached a daily rate of 200 rounds per piece, it is not surprising that everyone rapidly exhausted their pre-war stocks. Thus, in the first 120 days of war, the French fired off about 30,000 rounds of 75mm ammunition each day, an average of 10.7 rounds per piece, while the German daily expenditure was nearly 37,000 rounds of 77mm, 7.4 per piece, and 4800 rounds of 105mm, 2.1 per piece. Such rates of expenditure rapidly ate up existing stockpiles. Nor could current production do much to ease the problem. In the first months of the war French daily production of all types of artillery ammunition was but 10,000 rounds, and British productions not 35, and it was virtually impossible to increase production due to short-sighted mobilization policies which, in both France and Germany, saw skilled munitions workers called up with everyone else on the outbreak of the war. As a result, by the end of November everyone was very nearly out of ammunition. Indeed, in the B.E.F. ammunition became so short that the entire monthly allotment of 18-pounder ammunition was but six rounds per piece in December. This is one reason why the fighting came to a virtual end and trench warfare began.

CHAPTER VI

THE BATTLE OF THE AISNE

THE German Armies fell back from the Marne in good order. The Allies attempted to pursue. During the period 6 to 8 September the infantry of the B.E.F. had advanced only eight miles, their movement hampered by bad weather and bad terrain. Many British soldiers suffered from the change in weather, having discarded their greatcoats during the retreat from Mons. The bad weather also impeded efforts to use aeroplanes to scout the German positions. On the right flank the French Ninth and Fifth Armies were averaging about six or seven miles a day.

The Germans regrouped. Moltke, his nerves gone, was replaced as chief-of-the-general staff by Eric von Falkenhayn. Troops were ordered up from the left. The fortress of Maubeuge having capitulated, two army corps were released to the battle line. Falkenhayn hoped to restore German fortunes by reassembling his armies to strike at the Allied left. He wanted to do two things, first, to disengage the tired *First Army* and, second, to launch a counterattack on 18 September.

The *Seventh Army* came up from Lorraine, to join the *Second* on a line from Soissons to Reims. A new gap emerged between the *First* and *Seventh Armies*, which Falkenhayn plugged with a cavalry corps. Despite these changes, Falkenhayn was forced to cancel his planned attack. The *Sixth Army*, under Prince Rupprecht, moving up from the left, could not be fully assembled at Maubuege until 21 September. Bulow, who now commanded the *First*, *Seventh* and *Second Armies*, ordered an attack on the French west of Reims. Meanwhile, the Chief of Operations of general headquarters authorized the withdrawal of one corps from each

of the *Third*, *Fourth*, and *Fifth Armies* and placed them at Bulow's disposal for an offensive. These desperate and determined efforts to bolster German forces in Northern France were matched by similar efforts in the Allied camp.

On 13 September Joffre held a staff conference at his headquarters at Chatill-on-Sur-Seine where he discussed his future plans. Gen. Henry Wilson, a devoted francophile—and friend to Foch, attended, represented Sir John French, commander of the B.E.F. Joffre decided to launch a frontal attack on the German position. He felt that the Germans would be driven back to their own territory within three to four weeks.

von Falkenhayn

At this time the B.E.F. held a front of fifteen miles, deployed with I Corps on the right, II Corps on the center, and III Corps on the left. A passage of the Aisne was attempted on 13 September. Using boats and pontoons, some British units established themselves at Venzil, Vailly, Pont Arcy, and Bourg. The B.E.F. was in contact with the French Armies on both of its flanks. On the right Franchet d'Esperey's Fifth Army was held by German resistance, although his center advanced three miles north of Berry-au-Bac and the XVII Corps, on his left, crossed

Brunswick hussar in the new field grey uniform. The cloth cover for the busby has been pulled back to show the "skull-and-crossbones"-style insignia, often confused with that of the 1st and 2nd Death's Head Hussars.

the Aisne and advanced seven miles to Sissone.

On 12 September the German *VII Reserve Corps*, under General Zwehl came up from Maubeuge. Marching to Laon, it advanced to the positions held by von Bulow's group of armies, covering 40 miles in 24 hours. Observing the defensive potential of the Chemin des Dames ridge, Zwehl flatly ignored an order from Bulow to position his corps to the southeast, toward Berry-au-Bac. By 1400 on 13 September he had moved the *13th Reserve Division* onto the heights of Chemin des Dames while

Indian troops in France after their arrival in September 1914. Note drummer with slung bugle seated at left.

the *14th Reserve Division* deployed to the east, opposite the right wing of the B.E.F. and the left wing of the French Fifth Army. When Haig's I Corps attempted to seize the ridge, Zwehl was ready.

The B.E.F. had been making progress against stiffening German resistance. One brigade of the 1st Division even reached Gerny and La Bouelle, far to the north of the Chemin des Dames. However, German resistance became more determined and local counterattacks pushed back the thinly spread British units. The attack failed. The situation soon stabilized and the two armies spent the rest of the month engaging in local attacks, trying to push each other out of their positions with no definite result. The Germans could not be dislodged from the heights of the Aisne.

Algerian "Spahis" at Compiegne. High "Mameluke" saddles are still in use.

CHAPTER VII

"THE RACE TO THE SEA"

BY the end of September it was clear to both sides that the situation on the Aisne and in Eastern France was stalemated. On both sides the troops were tired, losses had been heavy. There was a momentary lull as everyone tried to recoup their strength. The commanders on both sides soon noticed that there was at least 170 miles of front extending from the Oise to the Channel that was occupied solely by clusters of reservists and cavalry, a military vacuum. On 27 September Sir John French approached Joffre with a request for the transfer of the B.E.F. from the Aisne to the left of the Allied line. This movement would cover the Channel ports and shorten the lines of communication and logistics of the B.E.F. Joffre said this proposal was agreeable if the transport to accomplish such a movement was available. He himself was already shifting whole armies from his right into that very same area.

Meanwhile, Falkenhayn was trying to tidy up his forces as well. Two corps, and much of Germany's heavy artillery, were tied up blockading Antwerp, in Northern Belgium, where the Belgian Field Army had taken refuge. This was a diversion of forces which he could ill-afford. As early as 16 September he had ordered that the city be properly invested. Its fall would release considerable forces and obliterate the Belgians as a threat. However, it was not until 28 September that a proper siege was instituted and the German heavy artillery began a systematic reduction of the outer works of the sprawling fortress-city.

By these decisions, French, Joffre, and Falkenhayn shifted the focus of attention to the far western stretches of the France-Belgian frontier zone. A series of attacks and counterattacks ensued, as each side moved fresh forces further west in an effort to get around the flank of the other.

On 30 September, Castelnau's Second Army, newly arrived from Lorraine, launched an attack in Picardie. A few days later an attack took place from the area of Arres. The light German forces held and by 7 October the lines had stabilized. But new attacks were already being made elsewhere.

During this period the B.E.F. had received reinforcements. The 6th Division had arrived in France in mid-September and the Indian Corps had landed at Marseilles, but had to be re-equipped before entering the line. As the B.E.F. shifted westwards, the British attempted to aid the Belgian Army at Antwerp. The Royal Naval

Barbed wire defenses in Antwerp.

Division was dispatched by the First Lord of the Admiralty, Winston S. Churchill, a formation consisting of a few thousand Royal Marine Light Infantry and twice that number of untrained naval personnel. A few armored cars accompanied this formation, which had no field artillery. The War Office soon dispatched the IV Corps, comprising the 7th Division and 3rd Cavalry Division under Maj.-Gen. Sir Henry Rawlinson. The corps landed at Ostend and Zeebruge between 6 and 8 October. However, the IV Corps had not advanced far before Ant-

werp capitulated on 10 October. With the Germans in close pursuit, the Belgian Army withdrew behind the Scheldt and later occupied a line on the Yser river from Dixmude to Nieuport. They were in position by 14 October. A determined German attack on Dixmude was beaten off by Admiral Ronarch's brigade of marines, mostly Bretons who could barely speak French.

The transfer of the B.E.F. to Flanders started in early October. The Cavalry Division—by now actually the 1st Cavalry Divi-

45th Rattray's Sikhs arrive on the Western Front.

sion—departed from the Aisne Front and traveled by route march. The II and III Corps were transported by rail to the vicinity of Ypres between 9 and 12 October, to deploy in the sector between Bethune and Ypres. II Corps then moved as far as St. Pol, by borrowing 400 motor buses from the French. The I Corps arrived on 20 October and occupied a position north of Ypres. Meanwhile, the headquarters of the B.E.F. moved to St. Omer on 13 October.

Faced with massive Allied threats to his extreme right, Falkenhayn decided that he would

British Naval Brigade in Antwerp with improvised armored cars.

One of the London buses used by British troops in Antwerp. This Daimler has been captured by the Germans.

German 21cm howitzer, used against Belgian fortresses and later in the war at Verdun.

use the newly reconstituted *Fourth* and *Sixth Armies*, transferred from the center and left respectively, to break through to the coast and eventually seize Calais. In order to accomplish his objective he called up large numbers of largely untrained recruits and filled out the thinned ranks of the *Fourth Army*. He tried to leaven these green troops with a few reserve

NCOs and reserve officers with prior combat experience, but their quality and effectiveness was low. During the campaign he was wearing two hats, being both Chief-of-the-General Staff and Minister of War. There was too much for him to do, he was running the war in the west and that against Russia as well. Despite many initial successes, the German Armies in the East

German third-line reservists. The cloth covers conceal the "Landwehr" cross on their obsolete shakos.

Russian lancers at the charge. Russians, Austrians, and Germans clashed in vast, but forgotten, cavalry battles on the Eastern Front.

had many more Russians to contend with. Moreover, the weakness of Germany's ally, Austria-Hungary, threatened the security of Silesia, as a result of a staggering defeat in Galacia in September. Falkenhayn also had to deal with the mind-set of both military and civil officials, all still convinced that the war would be short.

Credits for grain and fuel reserves were denied by the Minister of Finance. Germany was running out of trained manpower. Victory was proving elusive; they had gone past Schlieffen's schedule, without any indication of a French or British collapse. Falkenhayn hoped his new blow in Flanders would be decisive.

Russian reservists "flock to the colors." Their military escorts look suspiciously like guards.

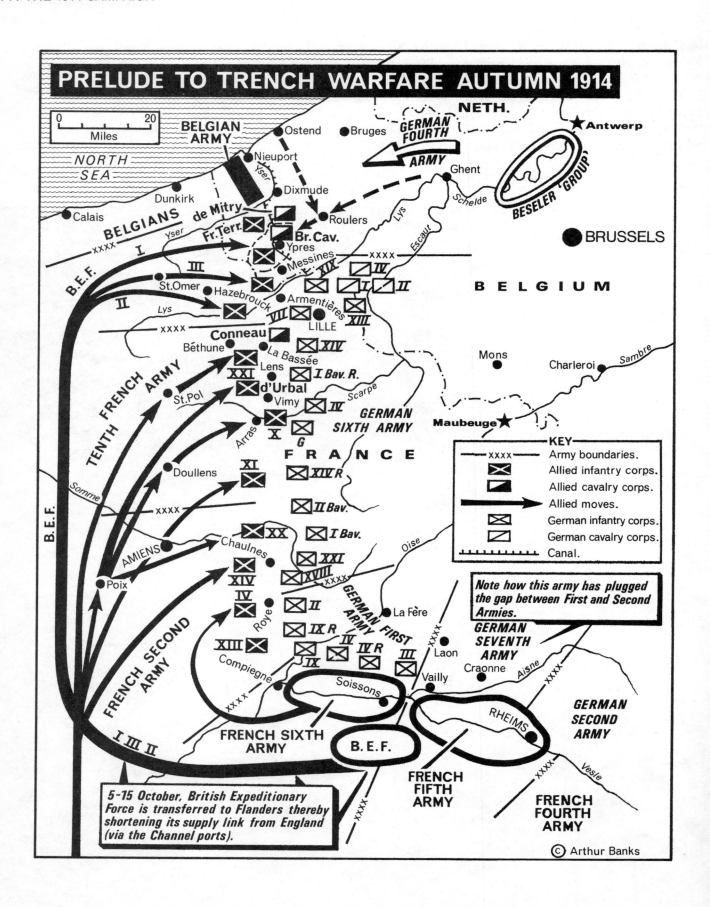

PRELUDE TO TRENCH WARFARE AUTUMN 1914

NETH.

0 — 20 Miles

BELGIAN ARMY

GERMAN FOURTH ARMY

★ Antwerp

NORTH SEA

Ostend • Bruges

Nieuport

Yser

Dixmude

Ghent

Schelde

BESELER 'GROUP'

Calais • Dunkirk

BELGIANS

de Mitry

Fr. Terr.

Roulers

Lys

Escaut

● BRUSSELS

Yser

B.E.F.

I

Br. Cav.

Ypres

Messines

XIX

IV

BELGIUM

II

III

St.Omer

Hazebrouck

Armentières

XIII

II

Lys

Conneau

LILLE

Béthune

La Bassée

XIV

Mons •

Charleroi

Sambre

XXI

Lens

I Bav. R.

TENTH FRENCH ARMY

d'Urbal

Vimy

Scarpe

GERMAN SIXTH ARMY

St.Pol

IV

Maubeuge ★

X

Arras

G

F R A N C E

B.E.F.

Somme

Doullens

XI

XIV R

KEY

II Bav.

XX

I Bav.

AMIENS

Chaulnes

XXI

Oise

XVIII

La Fère

Poix

XIV

II

GERMAN FIRST ARMY

Laon

GERMAN SEVENTH ARMY

IV

Roye

IX R

IV

IV R

III

Craonne

Aisne

FRENCH SECOND ARMY

XIII

IX

Compiegne

Soissons

Vailly

RHEIMS

GERMAN SECOND ARMY

I III II

FRENCH SIXTH ARMY

B.E.F.

FRENCH FIFTH ARMY

Vesle

FRENCH FOURTH ARMY

Army boundaries. ──xxxx──
Allied infantry corps.
Allied cavalry corps.
Allied moves. ➡
German infantry corps.
German cavalry corps.
Canal.

Note how this army has plugged the gap between First and Second Armies.

5-15 October, British Expeditionary Force is transferred to Flanders thereby shortening its supply link from England (via the Channel ports).

© Arthur Banks

By 12 October the British II and III Corps held a front in a semi-circle around the town of Ypres. It was here that Falkenhayn's attack fell. A series of small battles merged into one long struggle for the ancient town set in the water logged mud of Flanders. Initially the British attempted to advance between La Bassee and Armentieres, to be stopped by a combination of flat waterlogged terrain and the infantry of the German *Sixth Army*. The British then counterattacked to win the Battle of La Bassee. But the German *Sixth Army* was soon diverted further north. On 20 October it attacked the Belgian Army on the Yser. Both the Belgians and the French Marines at Dixmude fought steadfastly. The battle extended from the Sea at Nieuport to the La Bassee Canal, a distance of 45 miles. The Germans finally crossed the canal between Dixmude and Nieuport. The French reinforced Nieuport with an additional infantry division. The Belgians fell back between Dixmude and Nieuport, finally holding along the embankment of a railway line. King Albert ordered the dykes on the Yser to be opened and the land flooded. The German attack came to a halt and they later withdrew over the Yser on 1 November.

Despite the apparent growing strength of the German armies in the north the Allies chose to maintain their optimistic appraisal of their strategic position. The Allies still made preparations for a general attack on the Germans in Flanders. On 20 October, the very day that the British I Corps arrived in the vicinity of Ypres, elements of the German *Fourth Army* attacked the British II Corps, III Corps, and 1st Cavalry Corps deployed on a 16 mile front around the city. The British deployed their I Corps north of Ypres, around Langemark, and their II Corps west of La Bassee, until relieved on 23 October by Indian Corps while the III Corps and the Cavalry Corps, which was dismounted and stiffened by Indian infantry batallions, were around Messines and the IV Corps covered Ypres itself and the axis of the Menin Road and Gheluvelt Secorter.

The Germans were determined to break through and continue their advance to Calais and Dunkirk. The battle continued to rage back and forth. The B.E.F. was hard-pressed to hold its positions, but did so with heavy casualties. On 29 October the Germans were bringing in fresh troops from the Asine. The young, virtually untrained volunteers of the German *Fourth Army* who made up 75% of some units, were shot down in great numbers by the older veteran British infantrymen, who in turn died in great numbers. The Germans attacked the Messines Ridge, held by three dismounted cavalry divisions, and broke their line. Their attack was finally repulsed by the arrival of French infantry, who were thrown in to plug up the hole in the line.

Cossacks pass in review. A comforting sight to British and French newspaper readers but, even in 1914, the political situation in Russia was dangerously unstable.

The Czar observes artillery fire.

Russian bomber. Both the Russians and Italians went in for unlikely-looking long-range bombers.

On 31 October the Germans attacked with seven divisions against the British I Corps, comprising the 1st, 2nd, and 7th Infantry Divisions. Gheluvelt, on the Menin Road, was a key point because it occupied a high position overlooking the enemy line. The 1st and the 2nd Divisions were soon hard pressed. The two divisioned commanders, Maj.-Gen. Charles Munro of the 2nd Division and Maj.-Gen. S.A. Lomax of the 1st Division, met at the Chateau of Hooge to discuss the situation and coordinate their actions. The Chateau was hit by German artillery and both commanders were put out of action, Munro temporarily disabled and Lomas mortally wounded. All the officers attending the conference were killed or wounded, leaving both the 1st and 2nd divisions temporarily leaderless. The Germans broke through and cap-

German temporary shelters on the Aisne.

Royal Artillery brings heavy gun into action. The horses are of unusually heavy build, and the men wear non-regulation neck flaps in the summer sun.

tured Gheluvelt threatening the positions of I Corps. The British counterattacked using local reserves, beginning with the 1st Batallion, South Wales Borderers, from the 1st Division and the 2nd Batallion, Worcestershire Regiment, of the 2nd. Both units were understrength, the Worchestershires were led by a major and had only 350 officers and men. Nevertheless, they drove the Germans from Gheluvelt. The arrival of the French IX Corps, under General Pierre Dubois, greatly eased Haig's problems at I Corps. Both generals supported each other loyally. The battle was almost lost but the persistence of the British infantrymen and quick thinking on the part of the French Northern Army Group Commander, Ferdinand Foch, saved the day.

Canadian reinforcements arrive. Princess Patricia's Light Infantry, with regimental color sewn by the Princess herself.

On 1 November Messines Ridge was taken by the Germans in a night attack. The British still held to secondary positions until the French 32nd Division arrived and counterattacked on Haig's left. The French made little progress. By now the British salient had shrunk to nine miles. Losses had been heavy. The 7th Division fell from 12,300 effectives to 2,400.

On 6 November the Germans attacked again, near St. Eloi and came within two miles of the town of Ypres from the south. The French were unable to counterattack. The B.E.F. held its ground. By 11 November the German attacks on the French had failed and the German reserve divisions had been worn down. They struck the Menin Road with two regular divisions of the Prussian Guard Corps. The British line broke. Cooks, officers' servants, grooms,

17th Lancers get bread rations. The war has begun to slow down a bit and the mud has made its appearance.

Wounded German prisoners at Meaux. A captured medical orderly stands next to the young tree. The mounted French Dragoon has a khaki helmet cover as the sole concession to modern warfare.

drivers, and other non-combatant personnel were given rifles and sent to the front while the artillery fired point blank at the German infantry. Somehow the line was held.

When the battle was over—and it lasted from mid-October to the end of November—the Germans had lost some 134,000 killed and wounded, while the French had suffered 50,000 casualties and the British 58,000. Some British batallions were down to 100 men. Everyone had performed splendidly. The contributions of Foch as Northern Army Group Commander were considerable. Much of the credit for holding the Ypres salient must go to Generals Victor d'Urbal of the French Eighth Army, and Pierre Doubois, of their IX Corps, who loyally supported their comrades in the B.E.F.

New Zealanders on the march, wearing the characteristic "lemon-squeezer" hat.

Australians embark at Melbourne for European service. Patriotic feelings ran high, and nearby New Guinea was a German colony.

By the end of November the German and Allied Armies were beginning to show the signs of exhaustion. Since October they had been increasingly resorting to the pick and shovel and started to fortify their lines. Despite this, the senior commanders could not stop trying to win the war before Christmas. Joffre ordered an attack in Artois north of Arras, and a few days later another in Champagne, both with little success. little success.

The casualties of the steady fighting since August had started to show; there was a shortage of experienced non-commissioned officers and junior officers in all armies. None of the belligerents had made long term plans for supplying arms, uniforms, ammunition, and artillery. Many French reservists and Territorials went to the front carrying 11mm Model 1874 Gras black powder rifles, while many German *Landwher* and *Landstrum* troops were carrying 11mm Model 1875 and 1871/84 black powder rifles. The infantry of the British Territorial Force, which now began landing in France had to make do with long Lee Enfield Rifles of Boer War vintage which they continued to use for another year.

The next stage of the war was to begin. The belligerents would have to mobilize and train their manpower and organize their industrial and agricultural production for a much longer war than they planned.

The Cloth Hall, Town Hall, and Cathedral of St. Matin in Ypres, before and after.

CHAPTER VIII

CONCLUSIONS

EACH of the Great Powers entered World War I with its own elaborate plans. These finely tuned, complicated strategies, were really like one-act plays. Each presupposed that the war would be short. None looked beyond that first act. So the drama opened with a terrific first scene. But the rest of the act flopped and when it ended and the war didn't, no one knew what to do. Nor—despite the urgings of some visionary types like Kitchener—did anyone seriously revise their thinking for a long time, continuing to plan in terms of sixty or ninety day cycles, which rapidly turned into six months and then a year. Not until 1918 was anyone able to rise sufficiently above the errors of the past and prepare a final act. What happened in between was grisley and horrifying, unnecessary and wasteful.

There were many reasons for the failures of the armies of 1914. The changing technology, the increasing size of armies, the greater resources of nations, the enormous speed of communications, and the poor quality of the military leadership. Then too, there was the moral bankruptcy of the political leadership, which refused for over a generation to even attempt a peaceful resolution of the tensions dividing Europe, and which, abetted by pomposities of generals, firmly believed that war was a reasonable option. Once the armies began to march, none of these were so important as the failure of command. Despite mount-

ing casualties, Joffre persisted in pursuing Plan 17 in early August, while blindly pretending that an enormous German army was not sweeping through Belgium. Then there was Sir John French, who lost his nerve after what were essentially a few minor reverses. And finally, there was the Younger Moltke, who, through harboring serious doubts about the Schlieffen Plan, nevertheless merely sat quietly in a chateau far to the rear, attempting to direct his armies by radio and telephone, while sending junior staff officers to look things over in the field, when he ought to have gone himself. Of the three, Joffre was clearly the ablest and would last the longest. It was his imperturbable calm, his enormous confidence, and aggressive command style which were essential to the reversal of Allied fortunes in the Battle of the Marne. But calm, confidence, and aggressiveness were not enough to win the war. For that, new ideas were needed and new ideas were sadly lacking in 1914. In the end the Campaign of 1914 decided not who would win or who would lose the war, but that the war would continue. Because of the Campaign of 1914, Russia became communist, Mussolini and Hitler rose to power, the United States became a major actor on the world stage, and the European domination of the world began to crumble. Thus, in its very indecisiveness, the Campaign of 1914 proved to be critically decisive.

The Armies Compared, 1914 & 1918

Although everyone believed the armies they put into the field in 1914 represented the maximum possible effort on the part of their nations, the devastating experience of the war would prove them wrong. By 1918 all of the armies had changed and grown in numerous ways, as a result of trying to cope with the changing nature of war and the horrifying casualty rate. There are many ways to illustrate this, beyond the mere changes in weapons and tactics and uniforms. What follow are a series of tables which give some idea of the way in which the experience of war changed the armies.

Headquarters of the French Army

YEAR	PERSONNEL			HORSES	AUTOMOBILES
	Officer	Enlisted	Total		
1914	52	500	552	137	41
1918	500	1400	1900	200	120

The German Army

	1914	1918	RATIO	NOTES
Inf Divs	89	236	1: 2.7	A
Inf Bns	1241	3070	1: 2.5	
Heavy MGs	4060	30000	1: 7.4	
Light MGs	0	50000		
Cav Rgts	283	159	1: 0.6	
Field Art Bttys	633	2873	1: 4.5	B
Heavy Art Bttys	50	1660	1: 33.2	C
Mortar Bttys	0	281		D
AA Guns	18	2558	1:142.1	
Air Squadrons	5	400	1: 80.0	
Aircraft	300	4000	1: 13.3	
Engineer Coys	125	653	1: 5.2	E
Signal Coys	25	471	1: 18.8	

Notes: Figures for 1914 include *Landwehr* and other second and third-line components. Letters in the right hand column refer to the specific notes below.

A. The maximum number of divisions active at one time actually peaked at 240.

B. Includes batteries equipped with guns and howitzers of up to 105mm.

C. Includes batteries equipped with guns and howitzers of 150mm and above, including heavy seige mortars.

D. Includes infantry trench mortars of all types.

E. Figures for 1918 include 12 searchlight companies.

Machine Gun Allotments to Infantry

ARMY	PER BATTALION		PER 1000 MEN	
	1914	1918	1914	1918
Austro-Hungarian	2	24	2.0	30.0
Belgian	1	36	1.0	30.0
British	2	45	1.3	36.0
French	2	54	1.3	48.0
German	2	36	1.4	27.0

GUIDE FOR THE INTERESTED LAYMAN
Recommended Reading

Many thousands of volumes have been written on World War I in the form of official histories, memoirs, unit histories, local accounts, biographies, political histories, personal reminiscences, religious tracts, novels, and so forth. What follows is a sampling of the more interesting and more useful of these.

Non-Fiction: The single most accessible and most useful account of the Campaign of 1914 from the layman's point of view is Barbara Tuchman's *The Guns of August*, which, though over 20 years old, is still a valuable summary guide to the events of that fateful summer, despite a tendency to repeat and perpetuate some erroneous notions. George H. Cassal's *The Tragedy of Sir John French* presents a fine account of the operations of the B.E.F. from August of 1914 through early 1915. The best accounts of the French Army in the period are Douglas Porch's *March to the Marne, 1870–1914* and Ronald Narvey Cole's *"Forward with the Bayonet!" The French Army Prepares for Offensive War, 1911–1914*, the latter particularly valuable because it examines a number of the myths long held about the French Army. For the German Army Martin Kitchen's *The German Officer Corps* is of considerable use, as is Gerhard Ritter's massive *The Sword and the Sceptre*. Ritter's *The Schlieffen Plan* remains the standard work on that fateful set of documents, and is highly incisive in its analysis. Currently in preparation is Arden Bucholz's *German Military Planning, 1890–1914*, which is likely to be of particular value as well.

For maps Vincent J. Esposito's *The West Point Atlas of American Wars* and Martin Gilbert's *Atlas of the First World War* are particularly useful.

Many of the principal military and political leaders of the period left memoirs which are of varying utility. Of this considerable literature, none are as interesting or valuable as Edward L. Spear's *Liaison, 1914: A Narrative of the Great Retreat*, by an insightful British observer with the French Army; many of the most famous anecdotes of the campaign—such as Lanrezac's "No, they are coming to fish!"—derive from Spears, who went on to replicate his liaison mission in the equally fateful days of 1940.

Fiction: Although there were a flood of novels and short stories about 1914 during and immediately after the Great War, none now remain in print, the great literature coming out of the war deals with later periods. While the only recent work on the subject, Alexander Solzhenitsyn's *August, 1914*, deals with the Eastern Front, it is of some value for its explorations of military realities.

Journals: Most military and historical journals regularly treat World War I, and the Campaign of 1914 is by no means a neglected area. Among the more useful of these for the general reader are *Strategy & Tactics*, *Military History*, and *History Today*.

Film

A number of motion pictures dealing with the Campaign of 1914 were produced during the 1920s. Since then there has been little directly relating to the campaign. While original footage is rather scarce, several documentaries made about 20 years ago do deal with campaign and some of these are becoming available on video cassette. The more interesting are portions of Robert Ryan's *World War I* television series and several repackaged episodes from Walter Cronkite's old *Twentieth Century* program. There is, in addition, a film version of Tuchman's *The Guns of August*, which, unfortunately, spends a remarkable amount of time showing troops on parade.

Museums

The finest collection of 1914 materials is housed in the Imperial War Museum in London. Other collections of considerable value are those in the *Invalides* in Paris, which has one of the famed "Taxis of the Marne" hidden away in a corner, and the Bavarian Military History Museum in Ingolstadt. Though much of the collection is not on display, the War History Museum in Vienna contains some interesting exhibits, including the car in which Franz Ferdinand met his end, the gun that did it, and the uniform he wore.

Touring the Field

There are no guide books specifically tailored to lead the tourist around the battlefields of 1914, the Second World War being far more popular in that regard. However, in the immediate post-War period, the Michelin people produced a number of guide books to various World War I battlefields, including several of those important in the Campaign of 1914. While difficult to find, these are usually of very high quality, although wartime ferver shines through.

Simulations and Wargames

World War I has been rather neglected in popular wargaming. There are, however, several very good simulations available, not all of which are currently in print. The single most important simulation game of the Campaign of 1914 is James F. Dunnigan's appropriately titled *1914*. A highly complex, very detailed, and massively researched work, *1914*, may, however, be rather overwhelming for the novice wargamer. Less complex, but often equally valuable are Dunnigan's *The Marne* and David C. Isby's *Soldiers*.